A COMMON MAN OF THE GREATEST GENERATION

# Doyle Edward Bruce
## 1916 – 1999

**Edited By
Doyle Edward Bruce, Jr.**

Copyright © 2021 Doyle Edward Bruce, Jr.
Printed in the United States. All rights reserved.

No part of this book may be reproduced in any form or by a electronic or mechanical means, including information storage and retrieval systems, without permission in writing from the publisher, except by a reviewer, who may quote brief passages in a review.

Cover Design by Time Barber
Interior Design by Danielle H. Acee, authorsassistant.com

Paperback ISBN: 979-8-9857753-0-3
Hardcover ISBN: 979-8-9857753-1-0

Cataloging-in-Publication Data
Bruce, Jr./Doyle Edward
A Common Man of the Greatest Generation/Doyle Edward Bruce, Jr.
p. cm.
Library of Congress Control Number: 2022903026
First edition 2022.

# DOYLE EDWARD BRUCE
## 1916 – 1999

*This book is dedicated to those for whom my father recorded his thoughts on the most important aspects of his life: faith, family and freedom. Those are his children, Bill Bruce, Paula (Bruce) Ashworth, and myself; and his grandchildren, Ryan Bruce, Travis Bruce, Natalie (Bruce) Mihlhauser, Neelie (Bruce) Jones and James Ashworth.*

# PREFACE

Over two years ago, I began writing a book about my father's war experiences in the Southwest Pacific Area during World War II. My father left two records that form the basis of my book. Between August 1982 and May 1984, he wrote a chronicle of his life up to that point. I have left this account of his life mostly untouched (except for corrections of spelling and grammar errors) so readers can hear his voice. Fourteen pages of that document were about his war experiences. In 1989, he recorded two hours of videotape solely about his combat against the Japanese in New Guinea and the Philippines. While there is some redundancy in these two accounts of his war experiences, together I think they complement each other and enhance the story. Again, I corrected spelling and grammar errors. I also corrected a handful of incorrect dates or places to assure historical accuracy and I added a few explanatory sentences where I thought they were appropriate to clarify the story.

I did not excise the terms "Jap" and "Nip" from my father's account of his war. Considered offensive and racist now, these terms were almost universally used throughout the war rather than the word "Japanese" to insult and dehumanize a despised, yet formidable enemy. Other terms that may be offensive today also appear as commonly used in World War II.

I had planned to research archives of my father's infantry division, but the COVID-19 pandemic lockdowns and personal illness prevented travel to the sites of these archives. I continue to work on my longer book, but it

## A COMMON MAN OF THE GREATEST GENERATION

became important to me to promptly publish my father's own words about his life, perhaps because of those recent reminders of the uncertainties of life.

My father recognized the momentous changes that had occurred in America during his lifetime. He wanted his children and grandchildren to know what his life had been like throughout the 20th century. It is to honor his wishes that I am publishing this book. His observations of the hardships of life in rural East Texas, the sadness of the Great Depression, the brutality of war, and the resumption of his life after the war should be of interest to others interested in the thoughts of a common man of the Greatest Generation. His comments are often poignant and at times humorous. As I neared completion of this narrative I came across letters written by my mother who met my father shortly after he returned home from combat. I added her comments about life on the home front because her story completed my father's. Their story is just one of the millions that could be told by each man and woman of this remarkable generation of Americans.

Doyle Edward Bruce, Jr.

# Part 1

PART 1

# DOYLE EDWARD BRUCE

## August 30, 1982

This is the alpha of my life as best can be told of the memories that are in my mind. I have in my mind to write this so that whoever reads it may know what life has been to me, a common man. I have thought about this for many years and want to dedicate this to my beloved wife and my children and to my grandchildren.

How I would love to have a history or story from my ancestors, especially my father and mother. To decide how to write this has been given much thought, and I will try and relate this narrative in ten-year intervals. I am the sixth child of William Lonnie Bruce. My mother's name was Evie Mae Scogin Bruce. Papa was born in Rome, Georgia on August 5, 1878, and Mama was born in Appleby, Texas on May 22, 1885. I will give more detail on Mama's side of the family here because Papa's family tree is given much detail in J. P. Coleman's *The Bruces of Choctaw County, Mississippi*. Mama's mother was a Bullock, her grandmother was a Russell, and her great grandmother was a Crawford.

## September 2, 1982

My first memories of this life were in 1919 after World War I. I have a picture of myself looking at pictures Junyus Parrish took after he came home from World War I. We lived where the Lufkin, Texas sewer plant is today. Back then, we lived on a farm about four miles from town. That community was known as Boles School. And that road was the road to

## A COMMON MAN OF THE GREATEST GENERATION

Diboll. About 100 yards from the schoolhouse was a cotton gin. At that time, people farmed all of that land. About one mile south of the schoolhouse there was a large sawmill known as Hoshall. All that is left today is a millpond, concrete foundation and memories—some good, some bad. My father was a shipping clerk there for a while. My brother Victor and I had to do all the chores like cutting stove wood, which was quite a job for two little boys. But through those experiences of working as small boys, we learned to love each other and to share. What a wonderful father and mother we had, to work so hard to give us food and clothing.

My father would walk from Boles to Lufkin carrying his tools on his shoulder and work ten hours, then walk back home and do the chores around the house. Only the pure in heart would do that. All that I have of Mama are precious memories of how she worked to keep us warm and fed. She had to wash clothes in an iron pot and rub them on a rub board plus rinse them in a tub. This was done every week, hot or cold weather. If you haven't washed clothes in cold, freezing weather, then you can't imagine how miserable it is. At this time in my life, transportation was by train, a few cars and trucks but mostly done with wagons. In my lifetime I have seen in transportation the modes of moving go from walking and wagons to going to the moon in rocket ships. I've seen communications go from hollering to telephones, radio, television, and satellite. More changes have been made in my lifetime than from the beginning of time. Some things I say in this writing may not be in keeping with the time I am writing about, but I will say what comes to mind at the time.

In the year 1920, times were hard, and Papa moved closer to Lufkin. We called that place Feagin Hill, where Feagin Drive is today. Papa and Mama farmed, and he worked in town. He was a carpenter by trade. We also got our first car—a 1916 Model T Ford. It was a roadster, and it was impossible to get seven of us in it, but Papa solved that by swapping car bodies. At that time, the cars had kerosene lights. The lights weren't to see by, but to let people know you were on the road. I will never know why they had lights because the car made so much noise, you were heard before seen.

Back then, yeast bread was not too common, so it was a great treat when Grandma Scogin came. She would make lite bread. Oh, me! How delicious it smelled, especially to a five-year-old boy. At that time, in 1920, you could not buy goodies like you can today, and when Grandma made it, how special it was. This came to my mind thinking about that bread. Our cows would eat bitter weeds, and the milk and butter would be real bitter, but you ate and drank it just the same. While we lived there, my sister Hellen was born.

Also, while we lived there, my oldest sister, Willie Mae married Junyus Parrish, one of the finest, most unselfish men I have ever known. I still laugh today about him. He never did call Victor, my brother, or me by the right name. I think he did it to have fun with us. He looked on us, I hope, as sons to him because he only had daughters. He was the community mechanic, so two small boys were just right to hand him different wrenches and to get water to fill radiators. Mr. Ford never built a Model T that didn't leak all the water out in two hours, better yet fifteen minutes. The movie *The Grapes of Wrath* looked like an Easter parade compared to the Bruce, Barrington, Scogin and Pixley kinfolk when they cranked up the Model Ts for a Sunday visit or an all-day singing. Sacred harp singing is some of the most beautiful singing you will ever hear. They sing the notes from treble to low bass. And on those occasions, the women cooked the most and the best food. None of it had to be bragged on because it stood on its own merits.

About 1922, we moved to town, where north 4th Street and Chestnut Street intersect. This house was painted and had wallpaper. You see, poor folks didn't have painted houses or wallpaper. Oh, how wonderful it was to have screens on the windows instead of having to burn rags or cow chips to make a smoke to run mosquitos out of the house. I have often said

## A COMMON MAN OF THE GREATEST GENERATION

screen wire was one of man's greatest inventions. If you have never been plagued with mosquitos and flies, then try to live for just one day without screens when they are in season, and you can imagine how miserable life was then. Babies were the victims of mosquitoes. They would look like speckled guinea eggs from the bites. Everyone had malaise, chills, and fever from mosquito bites. The medical profession wasn't very good. They did all they could, but you usually got well of your own accord. Mother Nature cured more than the doctor.

About 1923, I had a kidney disease. Papa's cousin, Corbin Hood, boarded with us. He worked for the Southern Pacific Railroad building bridges, and he traveled all over the railroad. In his travels, he would get herbs of all kinds. Mama would boil and make a tea for me to drink hoping to find a cure for me, but all in vain. Mother Nature did it. There were cases of witchcraft or voodoo, call it what you will. They would try anything to heal the sick. For instance, a man who had never seen his father would blow his breath into a baby's mouth to cure hives. We wore *asafoedita* in a sack around the neck to keep from getting whooping cough, or kept a bean called a "buckeye" in a pocket to cure arthritis. I've said all of this to let you know how far medical science has come in the last sixty years.

Another thing that will interest you people of the future is the wages men were paid in the early 1920s. For nine or ten hours of work you would get $1.50 to $3.00 a day. In comparison, certain things were much higher percentage-wise. Shoes were $1.50 to $2.00 a pair. Shirts were $0.75 each. Trousers were $1.00 to $2.00 a pair. Groceries and household supplies were percentage-wise about the same. Now, in 1982, you can get much more percentage-wise than then. So in a great many ways, things are a lot better. Most people back then were honest and kept their word. You never had to lock your houses then, but not so now. I will talk more about this later in this writing.

I started to school in 1924 at Central Ward School. It stood where the Civic Center is today. Lufkin is 100 years old this year. Having the centennial brings back memories of the past.

Back to my schooling. Discipline was very strict. There was no talking in class, and you did not argue with teachers. He or she was always right, and the parents stood behind the teacher. In the first through the third grade, we had reading, spelling, writing, math, and music. After that, we added history, geography, English, and other subjects.

School started today here in Lufkin. I drive by our high school each day and the students have so many cars there is no place to park them. There's about one automobile to every third child, so you can see there has to be a large parking lot. I wonder if this kind of extravagance will last. In my school days, it was probably one car to every hundred children, so let's see how it is in your day.

It was time for Papa to move again, and we made our second move to the Boles community. I was in the second grade. The schoolhouse was a two-room building. We had two teachers, and they taught four different grades, so you can see that you got a four-year schooling in one year. I believe it was a good idea to be exposed to those different grades.

This has always been a funny experience to me. At Christmastime, the teacher let all the boys go get the Christmas tree. One of the older students brought their wagon and horses to go get the tree. It looked like Coxey's army that day, all of us boys going to the creek bottom for that tree. We cut a large holly, and it was a beautiful tree covered with red berries. When we got it in place, it touched the ceiling—twelve feet tall. We had to cut the top off so it could stand up. And this is the funny thing to me; we smaller boys had to climb the tree to decorate and put the presents on. Of course, on the day when the presents were given out, the same thing happened. We had to climb the tree to get the presents. The students exchanged presents. I remember what I got. Four firecrackers. I might add they could have been four sticks of dynamite from the explosion they made. They were "mega."

## A COMMON MAN OF THE GREATEST GENERATION

Our next move was back to Lufkin for a short time. Then we moved onto a farm below the town of Huntington to a community called Little Hope. And they called the name correctly because when we got there, no hope was in store for you. How sad it must have been for Mama and Papa to be in such dire need. But thanks to them and the Lord, they never quit trying or lost their pride. We stayed there one year and moved back to Lufkin. You can see I was getting to know quite a few people in all of this moving about. We did go to school in Little Hope—two rooms and two teachers—a man and wife by the name of White.

I'd like to tell why we moved to Little Hope. The year before we moved there, Uncle Will Pixley made a good cotton crop, so he needed people to help pick cotton, and there wasn't anybody to do it except children out of our family. Victor, Mamie, and myself went to stay and pick cotton. Uncle Clint Scogin's family, he, Aunt Gracie, Jessie, Benny and Emogene; Alton Scogin and Preston were there. Uncle Will had seven children of his own at home, and Aunt Ola had to do the cooking and caring for all of these people. She made beds on the floor for everyone and besides that had to haul the water in a wagon for all of this mob. Now that's what I call having a hard time, and only the pure in heart could endure.

At this time of my life it is 1926, and times were looking up. My mama had her hair cut off. Before that, her hair was real black and it would touch the floor it was so long. It was always so clean and shiny, and she always kept it in a "bun" as they called it then, real neat. I would like to add this; in all of our moving and hard times, at no time did Papa and Mama forget God or forget to teach us about the Gospel of Jesus Christ. It was foremost in their lives to teach us the Way and the Truth. They truly believed and lived it. (You shall know the truth, and the truth shall make you free. John 8:32)

I would like to add some stories which are true. The year I started to school, I would go home every day. We had a play period after lunch. The schoolyard was higher than the sidewalk, so I would roll off the playground to the sidewalk, then crawl to the corner of the street, jump up, and run home. Mama would get a switch and march me back to school. Mama and teacher would both get in a few licks just to keep in practice.

Mama was a really good seamstress, and I might add she could copy a dress or blouse for my sisters from a picture. Also, she sewed for some of the girl cousins, and all of this was done after she had finished her work in the home. She was a wonderful "Lady of First Class." I don't recall at any time she ever complained about her trials and tribulations. She was always encouraging us to hold our heads up with pride and remember God.

This story is true, and it happened in the year 1922. My oldest sister, Willie Mae, was married then, and she wanted to communicate with Mama every day. We were living in town in Lufkin, and she lived about three miles from us on what is now Feagin Drive. Mae had a dog named Rover, so every day she put a note to Mama on a ribbon and tied it around Rover's neck. Then she told Rover to take it to Mama, and sure enough, he went. Mama was always looking for him, but if she didn't see him, he would lie at the door until she saw him. Mama would read the note and write Mae, then he would take it back to Mae. This was done every day. This is true.

I remember this funny story from one Christmas. We always got some candy, apples, oranges, and nuts, maybe a toy or two. But that Christmas, I got a tin bugle and some firecrackers, so I decided to put a firecracker in the bugle to protect my hand and lit it. *Boom!* What a noise. All I had left for that Christmas was a big bang, the whistle to my bugle, and a small piece of tin with "Prince Edward Tobacco" written on it. How sad. That was the end of my musical career and Christmas.

Another thing I remember is when the circus came to town. Circus music has always been one of my favorites. Oh, how it would set a little boy's mind to wondering and dreaming about faraway lands where all the animals came from, and to this day, I love to see the trapeze artists perform.

## A COMMON MAN OF THE GREATEST GENERATION

At that time, 1920–1924, they came by train to Lufkin. The circus would unload their wagons, horse-drawn, and the parade would begin down Main Street. Everyone came to see the parade. Schools would let out countywide to see it. I will say this, a horse-drawn circus parade was much more exciting. Oh, that circus band, steam calliope, lions roaring, monkeys chirping, elephants and camels walking along in the parade… No wonder I never did grow to be a big man (225 pounds). All that excitement. It is time to move on to another decade. I will add more if I think it will be of interest.

### SEPTEMBER 31, 1982

Times were looking up for 1926. There had been more building, more automobiles, and better trains and tracks. The common man was seeing better times and he could do more for his family. Women were learning to drive the automobile, so that put them on the forefront.

I never forget the day Mama decided to learn how to drive. This was 1921–1922. We lived on the Diboll road that is now Southwood Drive. At that time, there was an open pasture where we let our milk cows graze. The weeds were about knee high, and so were a few stumps. Everyone got out in the yard to see Mama drive. Papa cranked the Model T using a hand crank to start the motor. He told Mama to drive around in the pasture but to miss the few stumps that were there. There they went, around and around, but sure enough there was an unseen stump, and Mama centered it with the front axle. So that ended the driving lesson, the Model T, and probably the family relationship for a few days. Papa could see the stump and was hollering, "Whoa, whoa," but it wasn't a horse they were driving. Papa took the axle out of the car, laid it on a flat surface, took a small sledgehammer and beat it straight, and the car was good as new.

Now to get back to 1926 and the next ten years. Things were about normal. Papa was working quite a bit, and we all had good health. We were now living up in the north part of town at Clingman Street and Rhodes.

I believe it was 1926–27 when they tore the old standpipe down. It was a huge pipe about ten feet across and maybe fifty or sixty feet high. This was where Lufkin stored their water and got water pressure. I was in the fifth grade when they tore it down. I could see them taking it down from my classroom.

Papa bought a grocery store and gristmill about that time, so we had opportunity to eat candy and apples more often, if we didn't get caught. Papa's feet got itchy, and we moved to Wells, Texas, store and all. I never forget the day we moved. It was one of the coldest days I can remember. We rode up there in an open Model T car and had to go into a cold house and try to stay warm.

I didn't know what to think my first day in Wells School. Every boy came in with a string with rat tails tied on it. The boy who had the most rat tails in a month won a $5.00 prize. More than one way to kill a cat: kill all of the rats. If you lived in Wells, you had to be accepted before anyone would play with you or invite you to their parties.

We moved to Wells in 1928. My school days in Wells are some of my fondest memories, and I made quite a few lifelong friends. In those days, a small town was isolated from other towns, so you had to make your own fun. I was getting old enough to notice the girls. It wasn't too long before I was going to the parties. All the people in town were good about entertaining us young people.

In the presidential campaign of 1928, Republican Herbert Hoover said, "We are nearer to the final triumph over poverty than ever before in the history of the land." The Great Depression came overnight. The stock market crash of October 24, 1929, happened suddenly and without mercy. People had overextended their credit—especially purchasing new cars. The Depression brought about desolation to the people who could not pay their debts.

It was one of the terrible calamities of this world. Poor folks lost houses, farms, cars, businesses, and worst of all, their jobs. It took about two years

## A COMMON MAN OF THE GREATEST GENERATION

for people to feel the full force of the Depression. By then, they had spent all their savings plus whatever they had to sell.

Hundreds of men stood in line to apply for a job, and maybe one or two men would be hired. The hourly wage was $0.25 to $0.29 an hour. Men, women, and families would be seen on freight trains going from place to place trying to find work. They would work at anything for any wages, or just something to eat for the day, and move on. Some would die, and the community would all pitch in and bury them although they didn't have anything, either. Hovels made of packing crates and tarpaper were called "Hoovervilles."

People who had lost everything, had no money, and had nothing to eat stopped at Mama and Papa's café begging for food. Mama fed many of them, selling everything on credit, never expecting to get it back, only hoping. I guess they gave to anyone who was hungry or needed clothes. Mama and Papa had to close their store and café. They were broke. By then, everyone was broke, working for ten to fifteen cents an hour, if work could be found. I have seen grown men sit and wait or walk the road trying to find work for as long as two years. But through it all, they kept a spirit that things would be better someday. I learned the way of life—the ways of the world—listening to those men talk. Some of it was good and some bad, but all in all, I knew what to expect when I was grown. My brother, Victor, and I worked in the fields chopping cotton, picking cotton, picking tomatoes, or anything we could do.

Gasoline sold for $0.08 a gallon, but there was no demand or any place to store it. The East Texas oil fields (the biggest in the world) were processing so much gasoline it was pumped into creeks. About the years 1930 to 1933, farmers started growing lots of tomatoes, so we learned to make crates to ship them in—half a cent a piece, twenty-four nails to the crate. The farmers who grew tomatoes would get half a cent to four cents a pound, and sometimes they couldn't sell them at any price. So, as you can see, it was a sad thing to work all year and not make enough to pay for the fertilizer. Everyone owed the grocery store. It went broke, and the store owner burned the bills and forgot about being paid.

Those who remember the Great Depression can never forget it. It molded their thinking for the remainder of their lives.

I saw one woman one day come running to town with her baby, and it died in her arms before the doctor could see it. It was so hot that day. How she must have suffered. She traveled close to four miles from home to the doctor's office. There was sadness everywhere, and yet people never lost their pride or hope.

Victor and I ran the gristmill every Saturday. I was too small to put the corn in the hopper, so Papa made a box for Victor to stand on to put corn in the hopper. I did all of the sacking. People used flour sacks or made a sack to put the cornmeal in. We got a sixth of the corn to grind it. Fifty-four pounds was a bushel of shelled corn, so we would get nine pounds to grind it. Some Saturdays, we would get two bushels of shelled corn. You can see we were busy little boys. Little boys would bring it to the mill on mule or horseback. They would be too small to handle a bushel of shelled corn, so Victor had to help them get it to the scales and weigh it. If we got caught up with the grinding, then we would have a marble game or maybe a fight or two.

This gristmill was behind a blacksmith shop, so we got to see them build and repair wagons and learned a lot just watching things go on. Sometimes it took every man in town to help put shoes on a big, wild horse or mule they used in the woods to bring the logs to the mill. Trucks were coming into their own, but you still had to have a big pair of mules or horses to pull the trucks through the mudholes. It brings tears to my eyes to remember how those teams would pull, and the men would strain every muscle in their bodies to keep things moving. No wonder they would get drunk on Saturdays. They had to have a relief valve.

All of the things we have today to make life easier didn't come cheap or easy. Men and animals died to let us have them today, and I never forget them as I drive through the country and see farms, roads, and railroads that were built by hand, ax, shovel, and dynamite. Men that did the dynamiting could look at a big tree stump and used just enough to blow it out of the ground and not into the air. That is where the expression "fire in the hole" came from. Everyone knew to look and see if it went into the air.

Speaking about roads, I can remember when you had to cross the Angelina River between Lufkin and Nacogdoches on a ferry. It was pulled across by hand. When they started doing away with one- and two-room schools and started busing, children did more pushing school buses out of the mudholes than they did in school. Progress moves on from mudholes to the moon and beyond. Dear God, how great thou art.

In the year 1929, Papa bought an Atwater Kent Radio. It had large speakers on it, so at night, if the power plant wasn't broken down, we had music, *Lum and Abner, The Shadow* and the news. People would sit on our store porch and inside until Papa decided to go to bed or the power plant broke down. The power plant always broke down just as someone was about to be killed. Now, after 55 years, everything worked out all right and we don't have to worry about the power plant going down.

I remember one day just at dark, they brought one of the town's men in to see the doctor. His leg was almost torn off and he was lying in the back of a truck. The doctor looked at it and said he could not fix it, but the man asked him to cut it off right there and he asked for a drink of whiskey so he could stand the pain until they could take him to Lufkin. He lived through it all and would get drunk every Saturday on his crutches and fall down and couldn't get up. Whoever heard him calling would know to help him up.

I remember one Saturday night my sister, Mamie, and all the other girls in town had a big picnic. Their boyfriends had a #3 washtub full of soda pop and ice—probably beer, too. They made a mistake and left everything in one car. All of us young boys stole everything they had brought and took it down on the creek not too far away. One boy, now Dr. John Craven, was always laughing, and you could hear him for a half mile, so the hunt was on for the food. Sure enough, they heard John laughing and knew they had treed the food! Talk about the ass kicking, laughing, and running. It took place that night. On Sunday morning, everything was back to normal. It was all in fun.

Another time, this same John Craven made a bet with Clyde Bowman that he couldn't run from Wells to Forest, another town about five miles from Wells. The bet was if he did run to Forest, John would push him back to Wells in a wheelbarrow nonstop. Clyde ran the five miles, and John pushed him back to Wells.

Mr. and Mrs. Craven had a large pond. It was all right to go swimming if John went along. It was hot one day, and it was too far to go get John, so we boys slipped into the pond not realizing Mrs. Craven could see us from the house. Anyway, she caught us swimming and was standing where our clothes were. She yelled for us to get out. I know she had a big laugh when about eight or ten naked boys ran across an open field to the woods. And lo and behold, the passenger train was going by. I hope some of those passengers still laugh about it.

I played basketball for Wells and really enjoyed it. I'll name a few of the teams we played: Nat, Cushing, Douglas, Neches, Ratcliff, Reklaw, Whitehouse, Zavalla, Huntington, and Indian Village. Those Indians never said a word while playing. They would just grunt "ough." But they were hard to beat.

Time was passing on, and Papa's feet were itchy so all the good times at Wells would soon come to a close. We moved back to Lufkin, and I started to school in Lufkin High School. I went to ten different schools in twelve years. Some of these were the same schools. So you see, I did well to learn to read. So be it. Life has been good to me, and I have no regrets. My last two years in Lufkin High were very dull. I wasn't allowed to play any kind of sports by state law. I graduated in 1935, but should have graduated in 1934. Wells didn't have credits in some courses, so I had to take them over

## A COMMON MAN OF THE GREATEST GENERATION

in Lufkin. Times were really hard, and no one had any money. Oh, how I wanted just a few dimes to spend. Who knows? Maybe those hard times made a better person out of me.

I must go back to 1933 and one of the most important days of my entire life. I went to hear Brother W. S. Moody, a gospel preacher. Of all the people I have known or heard speak or preach, he was the greatest. He once told me he could quote the entire New Testament from memory. He never opened his Testament but from memory quoted chapter after chapter. He would make the modern preacher today look like a novice. Only a few great men are born, and I was privileged to hear and know him. I must say, he made my life have a meaning and a purpose, and I hope to see him again someday in a better world and say, "thanks." And I would like to say now, without the help of a wonderful papa and mama, he would never have had the opportunity to teach me the way unto eternal life. Amen. I will have more to say about the Holy Writ later on.

While I was in Lufkin High, we would talk about what Bonnie Parker and Clyde Barrow were doing. They were in their heyday. They roamed over Texas, Oklahoma, Arkansas, Kansas, and Louisiana. Some more of the outlaws were Pretty Boy Floyd and Raymond Hamilton. They were all friends of Bonnie and Clyde.

President Roosevelt organized the "Tree Army," known as the "CCC," Civilian Conservation Corps. They were paid $30 a month plus food and a place to stay. They built roads, planted pine trees, built bridges, and built state parks and any other things they could do to stay busy. We can still see the results of it to this day in more ways than one.

I would like to say this about the president at this time and how I see it today. Franklin Roosevelt was from a moneyed New York family. When he was 29 years old, he was diagnosed with poliomyelitis and for the rest of his life, he wore ten-pound braces on his legs and was confined to a wheelchair. In his acceptance speech at the 1932 Democratic Convention, he used the term "new deal for the American people," and his administration was known for the New Deal.

The New Deal transformed American capitalism and made a start toward a welfare state. Government agencies to help the American people (especially young people) were created: AAA, CCC, CWA, FCC, FDIC, FHA, NRA, NLRB, PWA, SEC, TVA, and WPA. In 1932, all of these giveaway programs were started. Some of them were good, like the R.E.A. and other social programs, but they grew into a monster, and the structure of our wonderful country has slowly been taken away. This is the year 1982, and we are on the verge of a collapse in our government, as I see it. There are riches on one corner and poverty on the other. I am putting this in here so you people in the future can see we were aware of it at this time. Freedom is so hard to come by, and all people want it but will sell their souls for a mess of pottage.

## NOVEMBER 4, 1982

Today is the fourth day of November 1982, and we had our first frost. Such a beautiful day. My collards and turnip greens are looking good. I can see good eating for the winter. Better get back to the 1930s.

I stayed for a few months with my sister, Clifford Browning, and her husband, Richard (she called him J-Doll), in Baton Rouge, Louisiana. I was working for a large sawmill on the banks of the Mississippi River. I was making 18 cents an hour, nine hours a day. That was in the year 1935.

My next move was to the big city of Houston, Texas, on June 16, 1936. I started to work for the Southern Pacific Railroad, making 29.5 cents an hour and was damn proud to get it. Victor and I lived with our sister, Ruby, and her husband for a while and paid her twenty dollars a month each for room and board.

Another time, we lived in the Borden mansion built by the people who sold Borden milk. It would be hard to describe how gorgeous and fine this house was. Because of the Depression, the people who bought the house from the Bordens had turned it into a boarding house. It cost twelve dollars a month each for a room (two to a room), and meals were twenty-five cents. To ride the streetcar to work cost ten cents each way. That was twenty cents a day, almost an hour's work, but you could get a transfer from one streetcar to another and go all over Houston for a dime. Hamburgers cost ten cents, a Coke five cents, malted milk ten cents, beer ten cents a bottle, gasoline was eight to twelve cents a gallon, and, if you could afford it, a new Ford or Chevrolet was about $500, less whatever you had put down on it. My brother and I bought a 1936 Chevy and paid about $400 for it. There were a few thousand miles on the car. I was working days, and Victor was working nights, so the engine was seldom turned off. Things were looking up, buying a car. People were building new houses, buying new cars, new furniture, and clothes and could pay their bills. The economy was on the move, and business was getting better. People were smiling and laughing again, so you can see things are not bad for always. This about tells my life in the second decade. I will add more to this decade as I think of it.

## NOVEMBER 9, 1982

Today is my wedding anniversary, November 9, 1982. I've been married thirty-seven years to my wonderful wife, Helen. Better get back to 1937. In that year, we had a recession but it didn't last too long, and things got back to normal. I got a raise in pay. I was now making 33.5 cents an hour. I was working on the rip track at the Englewood Yard in Houston. We were repairing boxcars and also building new ones. I was doing really well. It cost me twenty-one dollars a month for a room and my meals, so you can see I had about thirty dollars left over to spend on clothes and laundry and myself.

I always loved steam engines that pulled the train. Those engines seemed to be alive to me, and they were so huge, and yet they would run a hundred miles an hour. To hear a steam engine blow his whistle today and to see the steam coming from the pistons, would be a great thrill to me. Engineers and firemen would always wave at people as they went by. If you lived close to the track and he got to know you, the engineer would blow his whistle just to say hello.

I had a chance to go to the Fulton Yard on Hardy Street, so I left the Englewood Yard. There we repaired the locomotives and serviced them for each day. I was working in the oil house and got to see the engines all I wanted to. I never lost my desire to run one. I had a chance to move up, so I started to work in the main warehouse. I was issuing parts for everything the railroad would repair and I got another raise to 39.5 cents an hour, making almost twenty dollars a week.

Business was good, but the dark clouds of war were on the horizon. The draft started, and men were being drafted for one year, but that didn't last long before men were being drafted for the duration of the war. I got a notice to report to the draft board early in 1941 and to have my business in order so I could be called at any time. I worked until September and took the examination so I could leave on October 6, 1941. I was making twenty-one dollars a month in the Army, and they deducted the cost of my life insurance and laundry. I came home to say goodbye to everyone. It was a sad day when I had to say goodbye to Papa and Mama. It was getting worse day by day, and we all knew that America would be in before long. When I later had to say goodbye to my son, Edward, then I knew what my folks had to suffer, knowing you may never see them again, but our prayers were answered.

My great-great uncles John, Greene and Mack Bruce joined the armed forces of the Confederacy on October 6, 1861. Eighty years later, I was enlisted to the day and my daughter was born on October 6, 1953.

Getting back to 1941, Victor and his wife, Sue, took me to the train to go to San Antonio. I stayed there ten days and was sent to Camp Roberts, California, for training. There were 90,000 men being trained there.

## A COMMON MAN OF THE GREATEST GENERATION

Almost eleven months after his third term began, President Roosevelt was informed that Pearl Harbor was attacked by the Japanese—December 7, 1941. War was declared on December 8, 1941. We were issued M-1 rifles and ammunition and given orders to ship out from Camp Roberts by train to Fort Lewis, Washington to join the 41st Infantry Division.

We were sent out on the Puget Sound to guard that coast. Oh, it was so cold. We had to sleep on the ground or anywhere we could find, but we survived, and no one was sick. We stayed there until March 1942, and then they sent us to San Francisco to get aboard ships to the South Pacific.

The ship I went over on was the *Queen Elizabeth*. I believe it was the longest ship ever built until this writing. Talk about big eyes; this country boy had them looking at that huge ship. It was 1,087 feet long and fourteen decks high. On the top deck, there were two swimming pools, tennis courts, lounges, and shuffleboards. Whatever your heart could desire for pleasure, it was there. There were somewhere around 13,000–14,000 men, including the crew, on that ship.

We were the first infantry division to leave the United States in World War II. To leave your homeland not knowing whether you will ever come back alive brings tears to your eyes, and to know that feeling you have to experience it. We sailed under the Golden Gate Bridge and said our goodbyes to America for almost four years. As I write this, my heart is made sad. So many young men never saw it again. They gave their lives so that we could have freedom. So, to the future generation or whoever may read this writing, keep your freedom. Never sell your country out. The older I get the more precious liberty is.

We left San Francisco on March 19, 1942. We landed in Sydney, Australia, on April 6, 1942. Sydney harbor was a beautiful sight. My battalion was lucky. We rode a train to Seymour, Australia, about fifty miles north of Melbourne, Australia. The rest of the division went by ship to Melbourne, then by train to Seymour. We had some training at Seymour and were allowed to go to Melbourne. It was a beautiful city, and the Australian people were the greatest. They opened their hearts and doors to us. I will never forget their hospitality. We had lots of beer and good food.

After a few months there, we traveled seven days on a train to Rockhampton, Australia. We had to load and unload our equipment three times because their railroads were different gauges (wide, standard, and narrow gauge) for different states. At Rockhampton, we had hand-to-hand training getting us ready for what was to come. On December 23, 1942, we sailed for New Guinea. All hell soon broke loose.

We landed in Port Moresby, New Guinea, on January 1 or 2, 1943. The Japanese were about thirty miles away from Port Moresby coming over the Owen Stanley Mountain Range, but before they could reach Port Moresby, they grew too weak to be of any threat. On January 7, 1943, we flew over the mountains to a place called Buna. The 32nd Infantry Division was already there, and we were to relieve them.

On January 9, 1943, we were baptized with our first combat. There is no way to describe the first day. Buna is about eight or ten degrees off the equator. The heat was hotter than Texas. Those poor northern boys, the heat almost killed them. Also the jungle rot, but we southern boys could stand more heat.

On January 9, we were going to cut the Jap's supply line but they cut our company half in two. All the next day and night, we dug a trench four feet deep and two feet wide to make contact with the rest of the company. The snipers were taking potshots at us all day. Every now and then, someone would be hit. The Australians, Americans, and natives all made a push and captured the trail the next day and opened it to us. Buna was a terrible place to take. A lot of men lost their lives there.

The 163rd Infantry Regiment (I was a part of G Company, 41st Infantry Division) was assigned to take a road to Sanananda Point where the Japs got their supplies at night. This was the time of year for the monsoon season. It rained every day, and the tide is high at this time of year. We were in water from our shoe tops to our shoulders all the time. We would cut limbs off trees and make a brush heap to get out of the water and try to rest. Our feet almost rotted off. When you took your socks off, some of the skin came off with your socks. To let you know how bad things were, I lost forty or fifty pounds in fourteen days. This is a guess, but when we returned to Australia, I was fifty-four pounds less in weight. The elements were as bad as being shot. We took Sanananda Point in fourteen days, so we got to dry out on the beach and let our feet heal.

I will only tell you about the places I fought at. I don't have words to describe what combat is like, but I guess the fear of the unknown is the worst enemy. The American and Australian soldiers are good fighters, so always remember that. The Japs were good fighters, but they had a different religion [and believed] they went to heaven if killed in action. We Americans don't believe that, so it made a difference in the way we felt and fought. When we took Sanananda Point in fourteen days, there were thirty-two out of 200 men left in Company G. Not all of the men were killed, but the elements and disease took their toll.

Our next move was to go to the Kumusi River; that was about twenty miles from Sanananda Point. We had to go up the New Guinea coast, passing through a village called Gona. The Australians who landed there lost a lot of men and killed all the Japs. We did not take prisoners except to get information. Otherwise when a G.I. took him back, he shot the prisoner, and reported he was trying to escape.

It took us about a week to get to the Kumusi River. We were ambushed on the way. We lost two men and several were wounded. They caught us in a river crossing and had a machine gun set up, so we had to go back or forward. Three men were trapped on the other side, but two of them swam out into the ocean and made it back. The third man was killed. This was at the mouth of the river. The natives that were carrying our supplies threw everything down and broke our radio, so we lost our communication with headquarters. The rest of the battalion thought we were wiped out. We made it to the Kumusi River and were relieved in a couple of days. The men that relieved us were caught by surprise, and the Japs killed quite a few. I never knew how many.

Our next move was to relieve another company at an airstrip and hold the strip, so we had an easy time for a month or two. We had to be sent back to Australia for replacements and to train them. Our regiment was used to teach other divisions about jungle warfare. Our Regiment (163rd) received a presidential citation for the campaign. One more thing about the Kumusi River incident: We were swimming (or, really, taking a bath) when an Australian and some natives came up on us. They said there was no amount of money to get them in that river full of crocodiles. A report later said several of our relief were caught by them. After that, we only got out about knee deep to bathe.

Before I leave this part of New Guinea, I must say that the natives that lived in the mountains were headhunters or cannibals. They would eat other people. We were given orders not to ask them for help. They would betray you and you would be eaten.

Just to keep the record straight, the Japs would eat you. I know because I helped bury some of my friends, and they had eaten their liver and the thigh and the meaty part of the buttocks. I saw the meat in pots the Japs were cooking when we killed them. So you see, war is not a glorious thing. The Japs did this because they were starving. Who knows? I might have, too, in some circumstances. This was put in this writing only to let future generations know what the soldiers in World War II went through. Again, I say freedom and liberty didn't come cheap. Avoid wars and seek peace if at all possible.

## NOVEMBER 11, 1982
### (Armistice Day)
Back to the subject in Australia and the training of new recruits. There

was nothing but hard training to get them in shape for combat and also to make us older men ornery and want to get it over with. I did get to pull guard duty in Brisbane, Australia, for three months. It was a large city, and there was something to do, pretty girls, and good beer and horse racing. Australians go for horse racing every Saturday evening. After the three months in Brisbane, I went back to my company, and in a week or so, we shipped out for New Guinea again.

The Division was split up. Two regiments, the 186th and 162nd, landed at Hollandia, New Guinea, and took that town, if you can call it that. Our regiment, the 163rd, landed at Aitape, New Guinea. It was a radio station and a lookout. The Japs had huge telescope glasses to watch over shipping lanes. These two landings were to get ready for the invasion of Biak Island.

The next objective for General MacArthur was Wakde Island. We made a landing at a place called Toem. This was on the mainland of New Guinea. G Company was left to patrol the coast, and the rest of the 2nd Battalion made a landing on Wakde, a small island about two miles off the shore of New Guinea. The Japs had an airstrip there. The island was two or three miles long and one mile wide, but the Japs had it well fortified with bunkers and trenches all over the island. It took several days to take this island. The Americans lost thirty or forty men, but the Japs lost over 900 men, so we had an airstrip for fighter planes and small bombers. Our planes were landing there a few hours after it was made secure. Those planes made you feel good to know they were there to fight off the enemy planes and ships. I have nothing but praise for the Navy and the Air Force.

Biak was the last stop for the Allies before the invasion of the Philippine islands. Biak was a coral island with mountains and jungle about two or three degrees from the equator. It was terribly hot, and water was hard to come by, maybe a quart a day. The Japs had the only water hole but the Americans were able to drive them back every day and get water. The Japs got water at night. Biak was full of caves in the coral, and the Japs took advantage of these caves. It was almost impossible to get them out. When this land and coral were covered by water, the ocean washed out caves at different levels. The more you pounded the Japs with mortar, artillery, naval guns, bombs, hand grenades, or whatever, the deeper they went, and after it all stopped, out they came and started all over. But leave it to an American soldier, and he will come up with the answer. We rolled fifty-five-gallon barrels of gasoline into the caves and shot them with tracer bullets to ignite them. That did the job. It burned all the oxygen out of the air, and it was so hot in the caves that they could not survive. Cruel, but so is being shot and dying. The terrain was so rough that it was almost impossible to get the wounded out. The terrain was a series of ridges almost straight up, and when you got to the top, it was about two or three feet wide and then straight down on the other side. I guess those ridges were about 100 feet high. It took ten or twelve men to get one wounded man out. You had to hang on to anything with one hand and pass the litter down with the other. They were strapped to the litter. How men suffer—I guess for greed in some fashion or another.

G Company was assigned to close a trail. It was the only way for the Japs to get in or out. Three of our rifle platoons were on the ridges and kept the trail closed. My platoon was at the foot of the ridges. We were to fire our mortars day and night to harass and keep them in the ridges. They were starving for water and food. What people don't know is that the Japanese would not surrender, so they starved themselves to death. We fired several truckloads of mortar shells at them. They sent out a suicide squad to stop our guns, but our riflemen killed them all. One had a message on his body to stop our guns at all costs.

I remember well that day and night. The best friend I ever had was killed that day: June 19, 1944. His name was Otis Belin, and he was from Houston. We went into the Army the same day and stayed together until he was killed. He came down from the ridges for something and asked me to go down to the beach with him to talk. That was on June 17, 1944. We sat on a tree that had washed ashore, and he told me he was going to get killed. He said his time had run out, and he wanted me to write his brother in Houston to tell him what to do with his insurance money. He wanted it to go to his oldest brother's children. His oldest brother had died and left two children—a boy and a girl—and a wife. That was the last time I saw him. He was killed on June 19, 1944. He was such a fine person. I sat up all night and wept for him, but that is the price we pay for our wickedness. Perchance God will forgive us at the last day. It is hard to understand, or it is for me, what a man is obligated to do for his government (New Testament, Romans Chapter 13).

The Biak campaign came to an end. The Japs were defeated, and the door was open for General MacArthur to keep his word, "I shall return." Heavy bombers could now fly to the Philippines and return. We knew that an invasion was soon to come. Our regiment rested and had a few days to get ready to land at Zamboanga. They sing a song, "Oh, The Monkeys Have No Tails In Zamboanga." That is true, some don't have tails.

General MacArthur made a feint that we were to land at Davao, so the Japs pulled all of their troops out and moved them to Davao. They left a small force at Zamboanga. It was a good thing, or we would have been slaughtered. The Japs had concrete bunkers to the water's edge where we landed, but no men to man the guns. I have never written this, but will say, thank you, Lord, for leaving those guns unmanned.

## NOVEMBER 12, 1982

There are two more places we landed that I would like to mention and that will bring my military experience to a close. This was a very important part of my life. I have only listed those places and experiences to give you an idea how things were for a foot soldier in World War II, and forgive me if it has been boring. I realize that I have used "I" and "me" a lot, but it is the only way to keep it true from my own experiences. The war was winding down. The Japs knew they were defeated. We landed on two small islands, Sanga Sanga off the shore of Borneo. There wasn't too much resistance. It was a naval depot and rest area for the Japanese. On these two islands, there were thousands of every size monkey you could expect to see. We stayed there a week or so and went to the island of Jolo. This island was where the Moros lived. Their religion was an eye for an eye and a tooth for a tooth. If their people were killed, then in return they would kill whoever did the killing. They either brought the victim's ears or his head on a pole to the town square. During the Spanish-American War, the Americans took this town, Jolo, in about 1898.

My last days of military service were coming to a close on Jolo Island. The day before I left, April 23, 1945, I had to go on patrol. I thought the Captain should have let me stay in camp that day. I left Jolo on April 24, 1945, my birthday. It was sad to leave my friends, but time marches on. I am sure I have left things out that should have been said, but I tried not to refer to certain people or names too often. It would cause confusion. As things that happened come to my mind I will add them. I was discharged from the Army in San Antonio in June 1945 and headed for home after forty-two months away without a furlough. Of course, the family was happy to see each other again. Everyone was rejoicing, and the food Mama and Papa had was what I needed to get started back on a new life.

The third decade is coming to a close. I believe it was June 28, 1945, that I met the most beautiful, wonderful girl who later became my wife. It was love at first sight, and in a few months we were married on November 9, 1945. Helen Slack and Doyle Bruce made their first home in Houston, Texas, and we have been happy all these many years. There is no way that I can express my love for Helen in words, but I have tried in so many ways. I know she loves me, and that is what counts, and every day we thank God for letting us have this beautiful life together and for raising our children.

## A COMMON MAN OF THE GREATEST GENERATION

To say more about our love for each other would become "mushy." A man's love for his wife is the secret of his heart and the treasure of his soul.

Before the conflict with the Nips, I worked in Houston for the Southern Pacific Railroad. After Helen and I married, I returned to work for the Southern Pacific Railroad in Houston. We stayed there for almost a year, and then we moved back to Lufkin, Texas. I began my apprenticeship laying brick for my father-in-law. What a grand old man he was. He taught me the trade, and I will always be grateful to "Papo" A. C. Slack for his training in more ways than laying brick. The only way I know to describe this man, Papo, is to tell where he got the name Papo. His oldest son couldn't say papa when he was small but said "Papo," and if you can imagine what a small boy thought when he looked up and said "Papo," now you know what kind of man he was. And the only way to describe my mother-in-law "Mur" is to say she is the one who made Papo. No man could have had a better father-in-law and mother-in-law than I did.

### JANUARY 18, 1983

I have been laying off writing since Christmas but must get back to this script. When Helen and I moved back to Lufkin, Papo had started a house over on Helen Street (although there was no street only a pine tree thicket). Papo gave Helen an acre of land where the house was, and we paid him $1,500 for the house. It was about a third finished. We started finishing it ourselves. You couldn't buy material after the war, so we bought as we could. Furniture was also hard to find, so we bought second-hand furniture. We had kerosene lamps, butane stoves, an outside privy, and we also had a small ice box to keep our food from spoiling. We would finish one room at a time and then move to the next room. It took us about six months to complete, but it was well worth it. Helen was working, and I never had too many days off from laying brick. I was making $10 a day then, but I was glad to get that. Helen never stopped working around the house and in the garden. You can make a good life if both of you try and pull together. We had a lot of company when we lived on Helen Street, and we enjoyed it and have lots of good memories. Papo, Mur, Mama, and Papa were still alive and gave us lots of good advice, which we took.

Things were the same from day to day until June 17, 1948, when our son, Edward, was born and Helen quit work to raise our family. She did a wonderful job with the children while I worked. Edward was such a joy to have around the home just as the other two were. All three children were born while we lived on Helen Street. William Scott Bruce was next, born on April 4, 1950. Paula Janice Bruce arrived on October 6, 1953, which made our family complete. We had to have a girl to go with those two boys. While we were living on Helen Street, the children were learning to do the things that would shape their lives from then on.

Everything was the same for several years watching the children grow—learning to walk, talk, and play together and making friends with the Read children next door. They are still good friends down through the years. No one could have had better friends than the Read family. Never a cross word. Helen was home with the children every day and teaching them to work and making a garden. That was a full-time job but we enjoyed every minute of it. I was laying brick every day I could. We would drive all over the country to a job, but we all had a good life, and above all, we learned to love one another. The way to a good and meaningful life is to work together, and Helen and I have always done that. We have always been blessed with good health and we thank the Lord every day for that and our other blessings.

In another period, 1946–1956, we bought our first car, a new 1947 Nash. It was green, and it sure was a pretty car. To ride in a new car instead of walking…what a treat! We paid for our house and finished it in 1947, so you can see things were looking up for the Bruces. In the year 1948, I went to work on the Lufkin Memorial Hospital, and I was making $20 a day. That was unheard of for someone to make that much money a day. The union scale has continued to go up ever since, and may I add that without the union, men would be making as little as could be paid. Don't be deceived.

## A COMMON MAN OF THE GREATEST GENERATION

Without the union, working men would be so poor and the rich would be richer. I know because I have lived under both kinds of economy. To have to beg for a job and to work for as little as the employer is willing to give is not much to look forward to. Never sell your soul to the company store. God forbid. Always give a day's work for a day's pay. If you are a slacker on the job, then you have stolen from the other man. So much for this subject.

The years 1946 through 1950 are called Baby Boomer years, and I am sure when you read this, you will see the results of this boom. I would like to see what effect it will have on history in the years to come.

## MARCH 23, 1983

I have been kind of slow in getting back to writing this. Today is the 23rd of March, 1983. The rain is coming down. Maybe we can get our garden planted. This has been a peculiar year as far as the weather goes.

There isn't too much to relate in these years [early 1950s]. Helen and I were working and raising a family. Helen's mother was having high blood pressure, and Helen was going over to her house to see about her every day. She passed away in 1958, and I lost one of the best friends I ever had. I will close this decade and begin the next one.

The next period of time is from 1956 to 1966. I bought four acres of land behind our house on Helen Street. It was at 1311 Slack Street. We started building a new house. We built it and finished it in 1957—a red brick. My brothers-in-law helped me lay the brick and my brother-in-law on my side of the family did the carpentry work, so it was a family-built house. My father-in-law built the fireplace. He was one of the best on fireplaces. Also, in this decade I built a few rent houses, which came in handy when there was no work and we had the rent coming in.

We still lived near the Reads. Our children loved all of them, and I am sure those people helped shape their lives. What a wonderful life these children had growing up together. Edward was in the high school band—lead trumpet player and captain of the band. It was one of the best bands

Lufkin ever had. Two years later, Bill was playing football, and they had a good team. His number was 73. Then two years later, Paula was in the drill team. I always liked the drill team. They put the spirit into the game. All three of our children finished high school and later finished college. I think Helen and I did pretty good to send them all to college. Also, when they finished high school, we gave each of them a new car.

## MAY 3, 1983

I need something to inspire me to get to writing again on this story of my life. This is the third day of May 1983. I have been in my garden this morning, working and cutting weeds. We had a nice little rain last night, and everything is looking good. I called Victor and Sue [brother and sister-in-law] to come and get greens to thin them out. We have had a very unusual spring. I can't seem to get things growing due to cold nights and cool days. Had a birthday party last Saturday night for me. I was sixty-seven years old. We had three more couples to have supper with us, Victor and Sue, my brother and his wife; Ford and Johnnie Barrington, they are cousins of mine; and Bennie and Belle Scogin, also cousins of mine. Helen made the most delicious supper, and everyone enjoyed it very much. Also, I went yesterday with my brother-in-law, Robert Smith, to gather mayhaws. They grow in the river-bottom land. They make the finest jelly man has ever smacked a lip over. Helen and I put the juice up last night.

I hope that in the future man doesn't destroy all of the wild fruit trees. If he does, what a treat people will miss. Wild plums are another fruit that makes delicious jelly. I am not talking about wild fence-row plums. I have two wild plum trees set out on Avranches Street. I hope they will be kept for future generations.

I have gotten off the subject. This is 1983 that I am talking about but will get back to 1956–1966. Things were about the same from day to day with Helen and me. I was working every day, and she was working at home keeping everything in order, but we were happy all of those years

## A COMMON MAN OF THE GREATEST GENERATION

spent raising our family. We lived at 1311 Slack Street for almost twenty years, and our children grew up there. I could say things about our living from day to day, but they were the same. Maybe a little different. The economy for all those years was very good, and people everywhere were doing really well—buying houses, cars, and boats. These were the years of good times in every respect. I will bring this decade to a close and begin the next one.

## MAY 16, 1983

This decade, 1966–1976, were the years Helen and I began to think about what the future held for us and to think about retirement years, and at present, we are still thinking about it. Today is May 16, 1983 and it is really cold, unusual for this time of year. Getting back to 1966–1976, these were good years. All the children were in school, and they all finished college in this decade. I believe America changed its ideals about freedom for the people more than any time in its history, and it was for the worst. We lost sight of morals and of God, and in those years, the decay of our government began. How true it is that the love of money is the root of all kinds of evil. Everyone was working that wanted to work and doing really well, but their goal was in the wrong direction, and I don't exclude myself. In those years, we saw old-fashioned grocery stores change to supermarkets that sell everything—grocery items, drugs, toys, clothing, hardware, produce, vegetables, and meat. The only thing they didn't sell was caskets.

## MAY 20, 1983

Today, May 20, 1983, is a cool, rainy day, and we are under a tornado watch until 10:00. It rained a little over three inches last night. Back to the 1966–1976 years. Lufkin did a lot of growing. Two malls were built and a new hospital and airport, but the airport never seemed to get off the ground. It was built for the rich and industry to use, but the poor taxpayer was the one to pay for it. Lufkin built a zoo in those years, and I must say it is nice for a town this small to have a zoo for children to see all different kinds of animals.

## June 15, 1983

Today is June 15, 1983, and I must say this. I had a visitor come and spend June 6–9 with us. Jim Perkins, the cook for G Company, 163rd Infantry Regiment, came to see us. It had been thirty-eight years since we had seen each other, and we really enjoyed the visit. He baked us some butterfly rolls and date cookies for old-time's sake. Of course, we talked about the war. It brought back memories—the good and the sad—but that is what life is made of, memories and hope.

Back to the 1966–1976 years. Prosperity was good, although I think it was false, and now we are paying for it. In this decade, we went to the moon and outer space, and it makes one wonder what the future holds for mankind. Will we go to the distant stars and out of this universe? How beautiful this country must have been 200 years ago. How beautiful it was until God let mankind set his own destiny and waste its beauty. I will close out this decade, 1966–1976. Life was routine—working, saving, and letting the children grow up. They were all good years.

I will start the next decade, 1976 until who knows when, and I will kind of ramble and say what comes to mind. We moved into our home in 1978 at 108 Avranches, Lufkin, Texas. I had my garden cleared before we moved, and it is in a perfect place. As I write this, I look out and watch it grow. Although this year has not been a very good growing season, these fresh vegetables taste so good. It won't be too long before we put up for winter.

## October 8, 1983

This is October 8, 1983, and that time has already passed for putting up for winter. We had a very good year and have plenty canned and in the freezer. I have a man with a big tractor coming next week to turn all the green weeds and grass under so I can plant my fall greens.

We had a bad storm this year on the Gulf Coast. It did lots of damage in Houston and the surrounding country. Also, the war clouds are gathering. It seems as if the world over is getting ready. It reminds me of World War II. They are getting the stage set, so it will be here soon. I have decided that wars are planned to help the economy and the rich men. I just might as well say it. You never see a rich man in combat. He sees that he or his children get the choice spots. I made it a point the other day and went to the cemetery to see how many flags were on the graves of the rich. There were very few, but the poor man's side had plenty of flags for veterans. I am afraid America will have a hard time getting men to fight the next war. Young people are not as ignorant as I was.

Don't get me wrong. I have no regrets, but I can see the whole picture now. I would still serve in the armed forces if it was to save this wonderful country, but to make the rich richer is for the birds. How sad that America the beautiful and the land of the free is standing on the brink of destruction. It reminds me of the Bible and Babylon: "How great the fall." I am praying that God will see fit to let us survive. Last week, on October 6 or 7, 1983, Russia shot down a Boeing 747 Korean plane, killing 269 people of which fifty-one were Americans. One of them was a United States senator.

## MAY 15, 1984

Time has passed, and here it is Tuesday, May 15, 1984. I glanced over what I have written, so I must get my thoughts together and finish this. I had my sixty-eighth birthday on April 24, so if I make any mistakes, I can always blame it on old age. Paula is ready to type this up for me and do some correcting in my spelling. Helen will love to proofread it for me before Paula gets it.

Seems like I talk about gardens quite a bit. Mine is real pretty this spring. My tomatoes and corn are pretty. I will name the kind of peas I have planted: black crowders, silver skins, and big boys. No telling what names the future will call them. The names of the tomatoes are big boys, better girls, and just plain tomatoes. I am looking for my twin grandsons to visit next week, Ryan and Travis. Hope I can have plenty of vegetables for them. Grandmother Helen loves to cook special things for them, and they always say, "Grandmother, you can cook better than anyone." We eat good when they are here.

This morning, I will say what comes to mind. Russia has boycotted the Olympic Games in Los Angeles this year. Also, we are having a lot of transplants of hearts and kidneys. I thought you might like to know that this all started in the last twenty years. Can you imagine they are giving birth certificates to little girls for a Cabbage Patch doll? They have messed up social security. I hope you people in the 2000s will know what social security is all about when you read this. If you don't know about it, get a history book and read about it. It was the greatest thing ever for old people.

There sure is some beautiful music coming from our radio this morning. We are looking for some friends from Virginia to visit in a few days. I was in the army with Ross Brandt, and he's bringing his wife, Ruth. We visited them in 1983 and had a wonderful time. They live in Ridgeway, Virginia. We are hoping to go to Portland, Oregon, this year to a 41st Division Reunion. Will see old friends that I haven't seen in over forty years. You never forget those men who stood ground while you slept—not only for your life but for those at home and future generations to come. Never forget the generations before you who did so much to give us a good life.

# Part 2

# INTERVIEW

The following is a transcription I made of a videotaped interview with my father about his military service in World War II, conducted by my first cousin, Sally Slack Clifton, at Daddy's home in Lufkin, Texas on April 16, 1989. In addition to her interview with my father, who fought in the Southwest Pacific, Sally conducted interviews with her father, Albert Slack, who was a fighter pilot off an aircraft carrier in the Pacific, and our uncle, Leslie Slack, who was captured by the Germans after landing at Normandy and spent the remainder of the war in a German prison camp. We children of these three lived among heroic men and never knew their stories of combat until Sally recorded videos of her interviews with each of them.

---

**Sally Clifton:** First we want to find out what branch of the service you were in and when you were drafted or when you entered the service.

**Doyle Bruce:** I was living in Houston in 1936 up until I was inducted in 1941. I was working for the Southern Pacific Railroad. I was inducted into the service on October 6, 1941. They hadn't placed us at that time, and I went to San Antonio. I stayed there about ten days until they decided which branch of service they wanted me in. At that time, they were really wanting infantrymen, so I went to the infantry.

**SC:** So you didn't volunteer for that. They placed you where they wanted you.

# A COMMON MAN OF THE GREATEST GENERATION

DB: I didn't volunteer for the infantry. They sent us to Camp Roberts, California, for basic training. We were there about a month or maybe two months before December the 7th. And immediately on December 7, they started issuing live ammunition and getting everybody ready to ship out. On about December 10th or 12th, they shipped us to Fort Lewis, Washington, where we immediately got more equipment, and they put us on the Pacific Coast up on the Puget Sound Peninsula out from Seattle and across from British Columbia. We could see the lights from British Columbia. And it was colder than the devil there. We walked guard up and down the beach and other places. We were camped in a CCC barracks, which was tarpaper and had barrels for heaters. We stayed out there five or six weeks. They brought us back in. We then trained in Camp Murray out of Seattle. Then we started getting ready to be shipped overseas. Preparing for all this, we got equipment and had to climb the barracks steps to show we knew how to handle a duffel bag. We shipped out from San Francisco on March the 19th of 1942. It took us fourteen to sixteen days to get over to Sydney, Australia.

SC: Did you go on a troop ship?
DB: No. I went over on the finest and best ship that's ever been built.

SC: What was that?
DB: The *Queen Elizabeth*.

SC: You went on the *Queen Elizabeth*?
DB: Yes. It was a huge, monstrous ship.

SC: Wasn't that the sister ship of the *Titanic*?
DB: No. It was the sister ship of the *Queen Mary*. I'll tell you a few things about it. It had fourteen decks. It was like a fourteen-story building sailing on the water. From the keel to the mast it was 365 feet. When we went

under the Golden Gate Bridge, we weren't too far from the bottom of the bridge. We could see people standing on it looking at us on this huge ship. You know, very few people had seen a ship that size. It was 1,087 feet long, and I would say 350 to 400 feet wide. It had two swimming pools, tennis courts and all up on the top deck. It was the finest ship in that day and probably now.

SC: It still is, isn't it?
DB: Well, it sank in Hong Kong harbor. I've forgotten how many tons it was. I know there's never been one built as big. England had these two sister ships, the *Queen Elizabeth* and the *Queen Mary*. The *Queen Elizabeth* never made a maiden run. They ran it out of its harbor over in England or in Ireland, where they were putting on the finishing touches to make its maiden run, when war was declared. They brought it to San Francisco, and they stripped her down of all her furniture and put bunks in there. But in the hallways, they left all the statues and everything like that. It was beautiful. Of course, we overloaded the dining rooms. They'd feed us in shifts, 3,000 soldiers to the shift. They had two dining rooms on it.

SC: How many times a day did you get to eat?
DB: Twice. You got up early in the morning and maybe, if you were lucky, you'd eat around 11. Then you immediately washed your mess kit, got in line again and sat down. You'd be lucky if you ate again about dark.

SC: That was your first luxury cruise.
DB: It was my first and last luxurious cruise. But it was in luxury. There were three ships carrying troops running in that convoy, the *Queen Elizabeth,* the *President Coolidge* and the *Mariposa*. The *Queen Elizabeth* stayed slow, so the other ships could keep up. There were a few patrol ships escorting us. When we got across the International Date Line and close to New Zealand, the

## A COMMON MAN OF THE GREATEST GENERATION

*Queen Elizabeth* sped off on its own. We could feel it speed up and leave the other ships behind. They were afraid the Japs might have set up something where they could waylay it. There were somewhere around 13,000 or 14,000 men on it.

We landed on April 6th in Sydney Harbor. As we came into Sydney Harbor, the *Queen Mary* was coming out. We passed her in Sydney Harbor. We all waved. They were bringing the Australians home from Tobruk. See, all of the Australian men were gone fighting in other places. That's why we went to Australia so soon. It was to give the Australians some protection. They didn't have any soldiers there, and they started bringing them back when the Japs struck at Pearl Harbor.

SC: How long did you stay in Sydney?
DB: We just unloaded there in Sydney. They unloaded all the personnel and everyone except the 2nd Battalion of the 163rd Infantry. That's what I was in.

SC: You didn't get to unload?
DB: No. The longshoremen went on strike and left us on the ship. We stayed on there nearly all night. Early the next morning, the strikers decided to let us go ashore. The rest of the 41st Infantry Division went to Melbourne on small boats, but the 2nd Battalion had to ride the train from Sydney to Melbourne, which was about 500 or 600 miles. We got to really see Australia first hand. No Americans had ever been up and down there.

SC: Did you see kangaroos and all that?
DB: No. We didn't see many, but we saw some emus. They're big birds like ostriches. We got to stop at what they call stations where they loaded sheep. They always had a hotel and plenty of beer for the Australians.

**SC:** Did you smoke cigarettes?
**DB:** No.

**SC:** I thought everybody smoked cigarettes.
**DB:** I didn't smoke. But anyway, we'd clean out the beer or whatever alcohol there was to drink. They'd feed us. We'd never eaten mutton sausage. You know, they were in links and they'd give us a piece of bread. It wasn't too hot, I can tell you for sure.

**SC:** It was just food, huh?
**DB:** It was just food. Then we went to a little place called Seymour. It was a town about like Rusk, Texas. Maybe not quite that big. But those people were really nice. In fact, they were happy we were there. Farther up the coast, they were getting all their silverware and stuff that they didn't want taken by the Japs and burying it out in the country where maybe the Japs wouldn't find it.

**SC:** Were the Japs attacking Australia?
**DB:** No, they were in New Guinea. We had about four or five months training. The American soldiers knew nothing about jungle warfare, and we didn't have any jungle warfare training. Our training was kind of a makeshift deal because nobody knew anything about it.

We left Australia in December of 1942. On the 26th of December, we had Christmas dinner. You know what we had for Christmas dinner? We had some kind of sandwich meat. What it was was bully beef. That's what we called it. You know what the dessert was? Two Jawbreakers. We landed on the 29th of December at Port Moresby, New Guinea.

**SC:** When you landed in New Guinea, did you know what your mission was going to be?
**DB:** Yes.

## A COMMON MAN OF THE GREATEST GENERATION

**SC:** What was your mission?
**DB:** The Japs were trying to walk over the Owen Stanley Range and capture Port Moresby, New Guinea. Those mountains were supposed to be impassable.

**SC:** That's that big mountain range?
**DB:** Yes.

**SC:** Who thought it was impassable?
**DB:** The Australians knew. Papua was a mandate of the Australians. The Kokoda Trail was what the Australians wanted to use to go over the Owen Stanley Range and stop the Japs who were trying to come over it from the other direction. The Japs were on the east side of the Owen Stanley Range, and we landed on what we'd call the west side at Port Moresby.

**SC:** Now is that Buna?
**DB:** No. Buna is on the east side. The Japs were within thirty miles of Port Moresby. But the strain and the altitude forced the Japs to go back. Some of the Americans walked over the mountains, but they weren't physically fit to do anything afterward because it was 15,000 feet high that they had to climb.

But we flew over. At that time, America had no air force, very little—a few bombers and all at Port Moresby. But that Port Moresby airfield became the biggest airfield, I guess, that's ever been known because that was the jumping off place for the Americans, for the Australians, and the New Zealanders to go back and take the Pacific islands which the Japanese had invaded.

**SC:** Okay, so the Japs did not control New Guinea?
**DB:** At that time, they did. All that was left was Port Moresby. Just a small area around Port Moresby.

**SC:** Wasn't Japanese controlled?
**DB:** Yes.

**SC:** So y'all were trying to get them off the whole island.
**DB:** Yes. Which is a big island. In area, I'd say it's almost as big as the United States. General MacArthur had gotten out of the Philippines and arrived in Australia in March 1942. At first we were under an Australian general, General Blamey. We stayed under Australian command for six or eight months.

**SC:** How were the Australian men to fight with, and how was it to fight under their commander?
**DB:** Well, my observation was and still is the same: that the Australians are the best soldiers in the world.

**SC:** You think so?
**DB:** Oh, yes.

**SC:** Are they tough because of that country?
**DB:** Well, they're not tougher than the American soldiers. They're brave. The Americans, when they got in a fistfight with the Australians, would whip them, but I don't think they would in a gun battle. I'm not selling the Americans short. They're great. But the Australians, they were superb, fighting men. They had had three years of training and fighting in Tobruk and North Africa. They were better prepared mentally. You can take an Australian soldier and throw him in the Angelina River, and he'll swim out polished, slick, and shined. He's an immaculate soldier. Yet, he's a brave man, very brave.

**SC:** Okay, so that was not anything unpleasant then being under Australian command? Did y'all like it or resent it?

## A COMMON MAN OF THE GREATEST GENERATION

**DB:** No. There was no resentment or anything like that. They were proud of us being there because it was a fact that the Japs were going to take Australia if we hadn't been there and if America hadn't sent them troops and material. There was no other way. The Japs would have swept right in there. And could have if they had kept going. But who knows? They stopped. They were trying to regroup, but that was their mistake.

We flew over the mountains. I flew over in a little airplane. They took all the windows and doors and all the seats and everything out of it. They just left the pilot with a seat and had one man, an American soldier, with a BAR gun. That was the defense. That was an automatic rifle.

We sat down on the floor, one behind another with legs to the side of the man in front of you. Thirteen could fly over in that little plane. When we landed at Buna on the airstrip, there, the pilot never stopped. He just slowed his plane down and we jumped out. He went to the other end. There was no airstrip. It was just a clearing in the Kunai grass. He turned around, and they were waiting where they could put on two or three stretchers of the wounded, and he took off.

**SC:** You didn't parachute?
**DB:** No, no. We didn't parachute. He just got on the ground and we jumped out with all of our equipment, packs, and rifles.

**SC:** Throwing all that stuff out?
**DB:** No. We had it on our backs. You had to carry it on your back.

**SC:** You didn't have a great setup there. There was nothing there when you got there.
**DB:** No. Nothing.

**SC:** Just you and jungle and the tall grass and what have you?
**DB:** Right.

SC: Was it pretty at all?

DB: Well, you were too scared for it to be pretty. You could hear the guns shooting, and you knew in a few hours you were going to be there. Incidentally, it was right on the equator, you might say—four or five degrees off the equator. It was hot. And these Yankee boys—especially these Pollocks, and people that were fair skinned, Swedes—that heat almost killed them. Being raised in the swamps of Angelina County is why it didn't bother me.

SC: You were right at home.

DB: Yeah. We had alligator like hide. There were gnats and mosquitoes, mostly gnats. They called them sand fleas over there. They would eat you alive, just eat you up.

SC: Did you have any insect repellant?

DB: Sarsaparilla, but it didn't help. They gave us a mosquito net thing that slipped over your helmet. You tied it around your neck but you couldn't use that, so that was discarded about the first or second day.

SC: Why? You couldn't operate with that?

DB: Couldn't operate. You couldn't sight your rifle. You couldn't hear well. You couldn't see well. So all of that was discarded.

On January the 9th, we had our baptism of fire. All hell broke loose.

SC: Okay, good. We've got to hear all about this. This was your first combat experience.

DB: We marched up to relieve some men of the 32nd Division. We got up to right where the fighting was going on. They gave our company commander orders to relieve them. We were to push on to what they called Rankin Perimeter. My captain was Captain Bill Benson. "Wild" Bill Benson was what we called him. He was a great soldier.

## A COMMON MAN OF THE GREATEST GENERATION

The first day, the Japs cut the company half in two. The captain was across this Kunai grassland. It's more like sagebrush that we have around here. The Japs were concentrated across a trail. They had a machine gun set up, so we couldn't walk across to get back together. We had to dig a trench across there about 400 or 500 yards. We took turns digging day and night. The other half of the company was meeting us digging from the other way. Then we made contact.

We were out of the Second Battalion, four companies, G and E and F and H. H was heavy weapons. The other three were rifle companies, and they had mortars and light machine guns.

**SC:** Which company were you in?
**DB:** I was in G Company, 163rd Infantry Regiment. The terrain was so bad, the jungle was so thick, that you couldn't use mortars. But we still had to carry them in case we did need them. The foliage overlapped over us. If a twig happened to be in the way of one of those mortar shells it wouldn't get but about ten feet high, and you would be in the explosion rather than the enemy.

**SC:** They didn't bomb that place or clear it out any?
**DB:** No. They couldn't. The Americans didn't have any airplanes. Not enough to do any good.

**SC:** In 1942?
**DB:** In 1943. Early 1943. January '43.

**SC:** It was toward the end of 1943 when they started getting the Air Force airplanes.
**DB:** Yes. The latter part of '43 and first part of '44 they started getting lots of planes.

I wish that I had this little brochure they gave us. The main thing it was for was to give us a few words of pidgin English. In other words, food, water, help, American or Australian, something like that. Just a few words that these natives could understand.

Now the natives there were of a great help…friendly, and we used them for stretcher-bearers and to bring supplies and stuff in. The Army sent mules over there, but the mules' feet were too small.

The Allied soldiers called the natives with fuzzy hair "Fuzzy Wuzzy Angels" because they were the stretcher-bearers and were very gentle with our wounded. They could wade that mud and water and swamp and carry the wounded out. Sometimes there would be as many as 100 men being taken out on stretchers. And those natives would carry them out.

There were slick-headed natives that cut their hair short and lived in the mountains. They were cannibals. We were cautioned not to have anything to do with those natives because they were very treacherous. They'd kill you and would eat you.

And so would the Japs. They were cannibals, too, the Japanese. A lot of people don't know that. They were starving and under those circumstances they would kill you and eat you. I had to bury some of our friends. They cut this part of the leg, the big muscle part of the leg, and the liver out and cooked it. They had it in their pots whenever we went to get our men and bury them. All we did was just throw some brush and mud over them so the grave registrars could come in and pick up the bodies and take them to higher ground.

**SC:** Do you think it was the natives that ate them?
**DB:** No. It was the Japs. They had it in the pot right there where we killed them. Later on, we caught them eating people. In fact, I have a record of it in *The Jungleer* where Dr. Holcomb from Enid, Oklahoma, wrote about it. I was talking to him about it, and he was very interested in it, and he told

me, yes, it was human flesh. I told him I'd gone out with three or four men to bury those fellows, and he wanted to know everything about it. He said it's recorded in Washington, D.C. He was a doctor, so he had to turn in all these records and recorded all of that. He had written a letter to his wife and told her about those Japs eating those American soldiers.

We'll get off of the natives now and get along with it.

SC: Yeah. What are you doing now?
DB: We had orders to go through a hospital. At that time, we had run out of quinine. That was before Atabrine was invented. We didn't have it.

SC: Is that for malaria?
DB: That's for malaria. But when we got near Sanananda Point, about a mile from the seashore, we came upon a Jap hospital. I'll tell you this, whether you want to hear it or not. I might as tell you what war was like.

SC: That's what I want to know.
DB: Well, we pushed through this hospital and killed sick, wounded, whatever. We just killed them. Just got rid of them.

SC: It was a Japanese hospital?
DB: Yes, and it was about knee-deep in water and mud.

We took no prisoners, and the Japs took no prisoners. If HQ wanted one for questioning, then we would save one. Other than that, we killed them because we couldn't take care of them. We couldn't waste the men to guard them. Over in that part of the world, the terrain and everything is so bad. And the fighting was all done in small groups. Platoons, mostly, running those trails. We'd draw fire and try to find out where the Japs were. They were doing the same thing. Killing each other, you know. There were no set rules over there. We wouldn't take any prisoners because we'd just be asking to be killed ourselves. There was no place to put them. And the food. We had no food. Very little food.

SC: Well, what did you eat?
DB: Bully beef and "19 and 17 crackers." What they called "hardtack." It was stamped on the cans, "1917." That was World War I stuff.

SC: Oh, really. Left over?
DB: I guess.

SC: Did you ever shoot game? Did you ever see any game?
DB: There wasn't any game over there. I never saw any snakes, but some said they saw snakes. There were some wild hogs—kind of like these wild hogs from Mexico. We killed one of them and ate him. But after you got to thinking about it that hog, he was eating dead folks and everything. We had Australian bully beef, which was a poor grade of bully beef because they were in such a hurry to get us into battle. All the supplies we had were coming out of Australia. They had cheese that was kind of like rubber. It was made to stand the heat. You know, ordinary cheese would melt and spoil. They had it put up in little cans like potted meat comes in. You could take it out of the can and it was kind of soft, but it was spongy, more like rubber. And that's all we had up there for several days.

SC: I know in Germany when they were in prison camp, they talked about food a lot. Did y'all sit around talking about things like that and things back home? Were you just miserable?
DB: No. There wasn't any need talking about it. We didn't have it at this point. See, America had just got in the war. America didn't have anything over there except a few men and no supplies. Everything was going to Europe.

# A COMMON MAN OF THE GREATEST GENERATION

**SC:** Did it make you kind of wonder what you were doing there if everything was going to Europe?
**DB:** No. Actually, I never did fret about it or get disheartened. You knew you were over there, and you were either going to make it or you weren't. This was all done around Buna. The Australians were to take Gona. Sanananda Point was our objective, to take Sanananda Point. That's where the Japs were coming in with their barges and things to supply the Japanese soldiers at Buna. The 32nd Division was at Buna. We were supporting them on the outer edges. Then we took Sanananda Point. We rested there several days. We ran out of water. There was water everywhere and not a drop to drink; I'll put it that way. We had to put these little tablets in our canteens to purify the water.

**SC:** Was that a lister bag? Did you have a lister bag?
**DB:** No, we just had a canteen. A quart's all we had. Or a canteen full. One day I just had to have some water. Oh, it was hot in those swamps! Not a breath of air. Americans and Japs had fought to get across a stream, and they were shot and dead and they were still bleeding. But that was one time I just had to have some water to drink. Blood was running down the stream. I caught a limb and swung out past the blood to get some water. That's how situations were. You get desperate. And when a man is desperate for water, he's got to get a drink. We went on up the trail to Sanananda Point. And we rested there a few days—three or four days.

Then they asked us to go to the Kumusi River. That was a river big enough that barges and maybe a small boat could go up it quite a ways. So they picked G Company. There were thirty-three of us left out of a company of about 200, a little over 200, 207. Something like that. That was a five- or six-day march to the Kumusi River.

Let me back up a little bit and show what conditions were like. It was so wet, so muddy, and so much water, that we'd cut brush and pile it on the ground and then crawl up on the brush and try to dry out during the night.

My feet are still bad because of the fungus. When you pulled your socks off, the hide would come off with your socks. I remember it was about five or six weeks before I ever even changed clothes. We didn't have any. There was no way to get them there.

SC: When you changed clothes, where did they come from?
DB: They'd try to get you some dry clothes and something clean. Just like food. They'd try to get that in there to you. They brought it in at night on small boats.

On the way to the Kumusi River, we had two skirmishes. They attached H Company, which was heavy weapons. They attached a squad of heavy mortars. They went with us. We had about 100 carriers carrying food and ammunition, and radios and everything.

SC: Were they American soldiers or natives?
DB: They were natives. Fuzzy Wuzzies. They were the Fuzzy Wuzzy Angels. We couldn't have gotten along without them, really. It took us about five days to get to the river. On the way to the Kumusi, the Japs caught us crossing another river and opened up with machine guns. The natives were behind us in the middle of our column. We kept a rear guard. When they opened up with the machine guns and killed several men, the natives started running. They threw the radios down. That broke all our communications. We couldn't get word out. And nobody could get word to us.

They finally sent a boat to find us. It was some boat. It was a lifeboat that the Japanese had that had fallen off somebody's ship. I don't know if it was American or not. The Americans had put an outboard motor on it which was a very crude-looking thing at that time. Not like what we've got now. Several men came up to see if they could find out what was wrong. Of course they made contact with us, which was very good.

## A COMMON MAN OF THE GREATEST GENERATION

**SC:** Were things just day after day?
**DB:** Yes. Day after day, we were marching up the coast. Later on up the seacoast, we got to use our mortars. We could see the Japs. And we called in the Australian artillery. They could shoot about twenty miles with that artillery. We weren't out of their range yet. They had sent an observer up there to observe for us. He was very good. He'd hit those shacks and other targets. Really, they were straw. I call them straw shacks.

The natives built them on poles up off the ground, and most of them were built out in the ocean a little ways. Their transportation was by boat. They had these little boats with an outrigger on it that kept it balanced. You've seen them in picture shows. They were excellent swimmers, and most of them, wherever there were pearls, they would dive for those oysters. They would dive and get those pearls. They could dive under the water, and it seemed like they could stay under the water forever.

**SC:** I want to ask you, too. Did you actually come up eye to eye with Japanese? What were they like?
**DB:** Yes, I did. As far as a human being, you'd have to go back and check with their religion. You see, their religion was completely different from ours. And you take a man that is willing to die rather than surrender, he's a fierce soldier.

They dug foxholes. We dug slit trenches. They dug a little hole. They were small people. They'd dig a hole just big enough for their body to get in there. Then you could hardly throw mortars in on him. One man could sit there in a place that he picked out and cover the whole trail. We went by trails one behind another like ducks. There were no frontal attacks.

**SC:** Was it like Vietnam?
**DB:** Vietnam was more open and had more fields of fire.

## DOYLE EDWARD BRUCE

**SC:** Oh, really? More fields of fire?

**DB:** They could set up over there. In Vietnam, they had helicopters and everything. We had nothing but mortars, and if it was close enough, you had a little piper cub that would spot artillery for you. Other than that, you were on your own.

In that kind of warfare, you knew if you got badly wounded you weren't going to get out. They couldn't bring you out. They had no stretchers or anything to bring you out on. Now if there was enough room, maybe we would pull back and take care of the wounded. But there were only about ten of us out there on a trail, and if you got badly hit, they would leave you beside the trail with your gun and a canteen of water. Now they would come back after you. Medics or somebody would come back to you. The only medics we had were ones that could just tie up a wound or keep you walking if you could walk—keep you from bleeding to death.

**SC:** So a lot of people just died?

**DB:** Yes. A lot of people just died on account of being wounded. You couldn't get to the wounded. A lot of them would have lived, but you couldn't get to them.

**SC:** And you didn't have a hospital.

**DB:** Oh, no, no.

**SC:** It was just primitive.

**DB:** Very primitive.

**SC:** That's what made it so hard there, wasn't it?

**DB:** Yes. Like I told someone—I know I told Helen—I saw the beginning of the end and the end of the beginning. The beginning was these people, they were naked except for a G-string. And they lived strictly off of bugs, rats, fruit off of trees and whatever, and fish. That was the very beginning of mankind. And then the end of the beginning was when these people were overcome by outsiders. And now…where we were, they have high-rise buildings on the airfield at Popondetta. It was strictly an airfield hewed out of the jungle. There was nothing there except an airstrip and a trail to get in there and out.

SC: Don't you think they still have cannibals there?
DB: Oh, yes.

SC: That's not Borneo is it?
DB: No. I was at Borneo. But that's later on.

SC: I want to ask you, too. I know it's not pleasant, but I'd like to know what was the most horrible thing you had to see in WWII? What would that be? Was that in New Guinea?
DB: Yes. New Guinea was the worst place for a human to fight a war. General MacArthur said it was the worst place in the world for a man to try to fight a war. The elements were the things that would cause you so much trouble. The jungle. The rain. The heat. If you drank water, the natives had bathed in that river. You'd get the yaws and every kind of stomach problem. You'd have the flux and that kind of stuff.

SC: Dysentery?
DB: Dysentery. Just steady dysentery.

SC: Did you get to the end of that peninsula? That Buna peninsula?
DB: Yes. We took Sanananda Point, but now we're talking about going to the Kumusi River. It took about five days, like I said, to get to there. When we got to the Kumusi River, we had no problems there, and we stayed

about two or three days. This Kokoda Trail I was telling you about that went over the mountains, this river went up not too many miles inland and that trail crossed that river. And that's what they were doing. They were taking supplies to those Japs going over the mountains to capture Port Moresby. When we got to Port Moresby, I'm sure the Japs saw us. I'm positive they did, but they didn't cause us any trouble. And I'm sure they went to get a big force.

They relieved us at the Kumusi. They sent a landing craft up there to pick us up—brought in men from another company to relieve us. I believe it was L Company. Being as there wasn't anything going on, L Company got lax. And those Japs ran in on them at night and killed a whole bunch of them, but they sent reinforcements up there and helped them out. We were lucky. We had just moved out before they counterattacked.

SC: They retreated, didn't they? It says in this book when the Australians counterattacked along with the Americans, they drove the Japanese back over the mountains again.

DB: Right. That's what I was talking about. We were the ones on the east side. We had come from the west side and flew over the mountains. The Japs were in there. They had no planes to get back. When you cut off their supply line, then they have to do something. They have to have food. Food is more important than ammunition in a situation like that. So they were coming back. That's what they were doing going up this Kumusi River with these barges and things, trying to get food and ammunition up to them. The Japs were retreating back to the east side where we were now. They were now between the Australians on the west side and us on the east side. Together we killed a lot of them.

SC: This book mentions this Japanese general, General Horii?

DB: Yes. He drowned during that retreat. Now then, when all of this was taking place, if it hadn't been for the Air Force, we would have never made it out because the Japs were sending thousands of men, lots of reinforcements to Buna. The Air Force attacked them and kept a lot of them from getting to New Guinea.

**SC:** From where?

**DB:** They were coming in probably from the island of Truk or maybe from further up the coast of New Guinea, like from Hollandia. Truk at that time was their biggest naval, air force and supply base. It was 500–600 miles from the shores of New Guinea. It was still close enough they could fly their fighter planes in there and strafe and bomb.

Ships, soldiers and supplies from Truk assembled at Rabaul on New Britain Island to attack the Americans on New Guinea. New Britain was closer to New Guinea than Truk. The Americans sighted this convoy coming from Rabaul and attacked it for four or five days. That was a major sea battle, the Battle of the Bismarck Sea. The Americans never let up day and night with their bombers. We could see them going over with smoke coming out of an engine or two engines. If it hadn't been for the Air Force, that part of the world would have been lost at least for a while. Because the Japs were after it. They were going for Australia, if possible.

**SC:** This book I have here says MacArthur started airlifting 15,000 fresh troops to go in there. Do you remember that? Sometimes these books are not factual, they make up stuff.

**DB:** At that time, they didn't have that many troops to go in there. A regiment, I'm going to say, is 5,000 or 6,000 men, counting everything. We had the 163rd Regiment, my regiment, in there. The rest of the division, the 1-6-2 and the 1-8-6 Regiments stayed in Australia in reserve. They were flying in a few Australians, but like I say, right at that point there was no Air Force, hardly any. We had a few bombers and were getting more in.

SC: Did you ever wonder how you were going to get out of there if you stayed alive?
DB: Well, I wasn't worried about that, about getting out. I just wanted to stay alive.

SC: Were you sick all the time?
DB: No, I had malaria. Had it real bad. But they wouldn't let you come out unless your fever was over 103 degrees, see. You'd just have to stay in there.

SC: Did you have medicine?
DB: Just quinine. We ran out. We took that Jap quinine in that hospital when we went through there. Theirs wasn't as strong as ours, so we just doubled up on their pills. We did finally get a supply of quinine. And later on, I guess they were making or working on it, we got Atabrine. We didn't have any at that time. We got it about six or eight months later.

SC: Did you have recurring malaria after you got home?
DB: Yes. Lots of times. The worst thing I had over there at that time was dengue fever. It's a terrible fever. You can't even bat your eye it hurts so bad. Every bone seems like it's going to burst. But it wears itself out. But they didn't send you back, you just had to lie there. The thing is, when you have fever and if you can think about having a fever of 103 degrees or more and getting out there in the river bottom when it's the worst that it can be and lying out there on the wet ground, well, then you can kind of figure out how miserable you can be.

The weather conditions and all, it rained every day during the monsoon season. That's when they had those high tides. They called them "king tides" over there. It backed water up every night. In the lowlands, I'd be in water, at times, clean up to my neck in my slit trench.

## A COMMON MAN OF THE GREATEST GENERATION

**SC:** How can you fight?
**DB:** Well, you just pushed on. The Japs would be either moving out or moving towards you, one of the two. Very ironically, I was reading in the last *Junglee*r I got, something I already knew. I was in the 41st Division, the 163rd Infantry Regiment. Well, they pulled the Jap Marines, their 41st Division, they pulled them out of Burma and sent them to Buna. That was two divisions of the same number, 41st, fighting each other there. Of course, the 32nd Division, took a terrible beating at Buna before we got there. You'd go down these trails, and you'd see four or five dead Americans. The Americans always fell face first. The Japanese always fell backwards.

**SC:** Why do you think that was?
**DB:** The only thing I can account for it is the Japs shot a 25 caliber bullet The Americans shot a 30 caliber. They weren't as big or as heavy of men as we were. That big bullet would knock them backwards. They always fell back.

The Australians over there did atrocities. The Americans did do atrocities. The Australians would chop the Japs' heads off. And that's a pretty gruesome sight to see bodies lying there and their heads cut off.

**SC:** Did you dream about stuff like that when you came back? Do you still dream about it?
**DB:** I never did dream very much about it. I do every once in a while, but not too much. If I dream, it's mostly about the contact I have with these men now. We go to these reunions. But the living conditions and the food. Now this was all under the Australian command. MacArthur was still in Australia. There were only two American divisions over there, the 32nd and the 41st, and we were attached to the Australian command under General Blamey.

**SC:** Is this where you were the whole time?
**DB:** No. No. This is just the very beginning.

**SC:** Did y'all get the Japs out of New Guinea?

**DB:** Yes. After we came back from the Kumusi River MacArthur brought in reinforcements. They brought the 24th Division in there to relieve us and run patrols and things. Buna had fallen and Milne Bay. The Japanese Air Force wasn't very active. They pulled us back to Australia and let us regroup.

They sent the 1-8-6 Regiment up to Finschhafen. To a place called Lae. That's where Amelia Earhart took off from. That was the last thing known of her when she left Lae, New Guinea. The 186th stayed up there. We were back in Australia getting regrouped and getting new men ready, They used us to help train them, because we now knew about jungle warfare.

The first thing to learn is to build a perimeter. You put two men to the foxhole if you could dig one. If you couldn't, you just put two men together; you made a circle of foxholes. The captain and the lieutenant would stay in the command post [CP] in the middle of the circle. The Japs would try to break the perimeter. They'd get in front of you or come around you. The Japs were sneaky. They'd been fighting in Burma for several years.

The Americans, we didn't know anything about jungle warfare at first. We had to learn it the hard way. The Japs knew. They had shoes with the toes all together and the big toe out here. Well, they could climb those vines and up those trees. Some of those trees were 100, 150 feet tall. And they put snipers in them. If you were out in this kunai grass, they could see it if you just moved it a little. Then they'd shoot in that. And they could see you. That's one of those things they knew about jungle warfare. They knew how to climb those vines and things. Just fork that big toe and those other toes around that vine and they could go up a vine like you would a rope.

**SC:** I don't guess you could borrow their shoes. They were all too little.

**DB:** Yes. They were all too little.

## A COMMON MAN OF THE GREATEST GENERATION

SC: When did MacArthur come?
DB: He got to Australia in March 1943. We got there in April. He had to come by PT boat out of the Philippines. I believe he came into Darwin, Australia. Then he went by train into Melbourne. Melbourne was his headquarters. He later moved them on up the islands.

SC: And Eichelberger?
DB: General Eichelberger was there with us. When MacArthur got set up, so to speak, he took over. There was MacArthur, Eichelberger and another general. I'm trying to think of his name. Eichelberger was a three-star general. Four stars were as high as you could go at that time. Eichelberger was a field commander under MacArthur. He was in New Guinea.

SC: Did you ever see him?
DB: No. I never saw him. I knew General Doe. He was eventually general of the 41st Division. He was just a colonel when I saw him. They moved him up. He was just a colonel when he came up to see about us. He made general. They fired General Fuller, relieved him of his command.

SC: Was he not good?
DB: He was a real good man. He was a real good general, but he wouldn't run the troops in and just get us slaughtered. He'd sit back and wait and figure things out and make a plan instead of just rushing up on pillboxes.

SC: This says that New Guinea is the world's second-biggest island. I guess that would be about the size of the United States. This says by the time the Buna campaign came to an end, the Allied casualties came to a staggering 17,215. That's dead, wounded or diseased. It says the battle for Buna was as bad as Guadalcanal. It didn't get as much notice as Guadalcanal, but the fighting and the cost in dead was higher.

**DB:** It was worse. I read a book, the name of it was *Bloody Buna,* which said it was one of the worst battles of the whole war over there in the Southwest Pacific.

**SC:** You never got wounded, though?
**DB:** Yes. I did twice.

**SC:** Tell me about that.
**DB:** I haven't gotten to where I got wounded. We haven't even gotten out of New Guinea yet. We're just about 300 miles up the coast.

It took us about three months to get regrouped and train the new boys. This friend that comes to see us, Ross Brandt, he was one of the replacements. We became good friends and still are.

But anyway we left Rockhampton, Australia. I can't remember exactly the date, probably in December. No. A little later than that, probably in March. We made landings at Aitape and Hollandia. We're out of Papua, New Guinea now, and we're in the Netherland Dutch East Indies. New Guinea is cut about half in two into Papua and Dutch New Guinea. We landed at Aitape a day before the rest of the division landed at Hollandia. Our purpose was to take the airfield.

A real good friend of mine, Dr. Hargis Westerfield, he's a historian and our unit historian, goes to Washington, D.C., and reads all those records about our division. He's a brilliant man. He writes all the stories in *The Jungleer,* our division magazine. Helen has met all those people. She knows all these stories. She's heard them backward and forward.

Let me see. Where was I? MacArthur had feinted that he was going to hit a place called Wewak. The Japanese pulled their soldiers from Hollandia and they marched down the coast to Wewak—around 90,000 men. We landed at Aitape. The next day, the rest of the division landed at Hollandia. We had the Japs in between us. At this time, they were fighting for survival. MacArthur had started cutting off their supply lines. And now he had enough airplanes and all. Our whole operation was more or less like the Marines. Only, we didn't storm the beaches. We went in, but we didn't storm the beaches and just slaughter the men. What we were doing, we were cutting off the supply lines. Plus, everywhere we went in a few days' time, they had an airstrip for fighter planes. See, the fighter planes couldn't go as far as the bombers, and the bombers needed protection. These bombers were still coming out of Port Moresby. But the fighter planes, as we moved up the coast, they could protect those bombers longer.

SC: Couldn't aircraft carriers help? The Japanese didn't have carriers. Did we have carriers?

DB: No. The Japanese didn't have aircraft carriers there. At that time I don't know how many we had. I'll say this. When we landed in Aitape, I counted as far as I could see—119 ships in that convoy. And there were three small carriers. They weren't as big as those that your daddy [Albert Slack] was on. They were smaller. But they couldn't sit still. They had to be on the move because the Japs would attack them. The Army Air Force followed us all the time. Just as soon as we hit the beach, I'd say in ten hours, they'd be making an airfield.

SC: Were there Seabees there?

DB: Yes. They had Seabees, and they had Army engineers that built things for the Army. I can't remember exactly what they called them in the Army.

SC: Well, Seabees must be construction.

DB: That's Navy Seabees, not Army.

SC: Was that April of 1944?

DB: No. June of 1944 was on Biak. We haven't gotten to Biak yet. We haven't gotten out of Wakde yet. Well, wait a minute. I can look at this flag here. This was May the 10th, 1944. I got this flag at Aitape out of a cave. The cave was up on a high bluff. They were using it for a lookout. It was maybe 100 feet down to the ocean. They had big telescopes. They could see for miles. In fact, we got one of their telescopes. You could see for miles and miles. Your eye couldn't even pick something up, but you get that telescope, and you could pick up a ship going by out there. They were able to send messages back about what the Allies were doing—how many ships and things were going past or they hadn't seen any ships. They were picking up those things like that. But that was May the 10th.

So April was a month before that. We had landed there. Now, April the 22nd, we were pushing up. I've got a picture here. That's about all there was to it—a jailhouse. Here's where I got that flag, right over here [points to a picture]. The ocean was down below us, and they had a little trail cut in the bank. They just dug a hole in there. It was hidden, and they had ammunition and all of that kind of stuff in there to supply themselves and radio equipment and everything like that.

Aitape is not in Papua. It's up in the Dutch part. They had a radio station there. And this was a building where the Australians or the Netherlands had their constable. And we got money up there, gilders when they paid us. Before the war, they put natives in this jailhouse to keep them.

**SC:** When they would act up?
**DB:** Yes. They had these big coconut plantations. They'd get that hemp from the coconuts to make ropes, cargo nets, and whatever they used it for. And that's what these natives did. And there was one house up there all by itself for the overseer. He was the overseer for a territory as big as Dallas.

Now we went into a place called Toem, Dutch New Guinea, after we left Aitape. Toem was near the Tor River. We landed down below at Toem, and the 1-5-8, which was a regiment all to itself and wasn't in a division, landed at the river. There was an island, Wakde, off the coast.

## A COMMON MAN OF THE GREATEST GENERATION

That was a solid island of Japs and pillboxes. It wasn't very big. It was two to three miles long and maybe a mile wide. We killed a thousand men on that island. There was an airstrip. A bomber could land on it. That was getting the stage set for MacArthur. That was his toehold to go back to the Philippines. After we took that, we regrouped and stayed a few days and got cleaned up.

We left Aitape and on June 4th or 5th we landed on Biak. And my friend got killed June the 19th. I'll never forget it. The reason I remember it is because June the 19th here in Texas is Juneteenth.

**SC:** How did he get killed? Were you right there with him?
**DB:** No. I was firing the mortars. We had the Japs hemmed in, so to speak, up in the caves. It's usually everything if you get the high ground. You've got the advantage to a degree, but I'd rather be on the aggressive side than on the defensive side because the defense, he's a loser just about every time. But, anyway, Belin was on a patrol.

**SC:** What was his name?
**DB:** Otis Belin.

**SC:** Where was he from?
**DB:** He was really from Arkansas, but he and I left Houston at the same time.
He was a fine man.

**SC:** I bet he was. So, he got hit by a bullet?
**DB:** He got hit by probably an automatic rifle.

**SC:** You weren't with him that day?
**DB:** No. I told Sandra, but I'll tell you so you can get it on tape. Belin came down about the 17th of June. We were firing those mortars. We fired a shell

74

every minute, day and night. Never stopped. And that's the reason there's so many shells here in this picture. Piles of them. We had the Japs where they couldn't get out and get water. See, water was the main thing. When you run out of water, you're desperate. We were firing these guns. We had three guns firing down from the Biak ridges. The ridges there, you had to climb them like climbing a ladder. They were about 100 to 150 feet high. And when you got to the top, they weren't as wide as that table. Then you'd have to climb right straight back down. Those Japs had the high ground. But we had them hemmed in. And they had artillery up in those mountains.

**SC:** But they didn't have water?
**DB:** They didn't have water. On these Coral Islands, if there's not rain or some source of water, there's not much soil. It's just solid coral. Trees and things grow out of it and have made some soil up there but it's solid coral under it. You wear out shoes in a few days. It cuts them all to pieces.

Belin came down out of these ridges and he told me, "Let's go and talk." We went down to the beach and we sat on a log and he told me, "If things don't change, I'll get killed in a few days." So we talked. He told me, "I want you to write my brother. Take my brother's address and write him because I know I'm going to get killed." He told me what to do with his money. He said, "Take my insurance money and give it to my oldest brother's children," because his oldest brother had died and he wanted them to have that to educate themselves. On June 19th he got killed. And that was the 17th [when we talked], so he had figured it pretty close.

**SC:** Is it because he had to do all this climbing and things that were so dangerous?
**DB:** Well, I have a poem here that Sandra read. It's called "When We've Done Our Hitch in Hell."

## A COMMON MAN OF THE GREATEST GENERATION

As we are sitting here and thinking of the things we left behind.
We would hate to put on paper what is running through our minds.
We have dug a million ditches and cleared a thousand miles of ground.
No other place this side of hell I'm sure cannot be found,
But there's a certain consolation now gather around while I tell.
When we die we go to heaven for we done our hitch in <u>HELL</u>.

We built a million kitchens where the cooks could stew our beans.
We stood a million guard mounts; we cleaned the camps' latrines.
We washed a million dishes; we peeled a million spuds.
We killed a million snakes and ants that tried to steal our grub.
But when our work on earth is over then our friends on earth can tell.
When we died we went to heaven for we done our hitch in <u>HELL</u>.

We heard a million ack-ack bursts above us in the sky.
When we went whirling for the slit trenches when the daisy mowers fly.
Put out those lights and cigarettes we could hear the sergeant yell.
This is not a picnic, but another hitch in <u>HELL</u>.

When our final taps are sounded and we lay aside life's care.
When we stand our last inspection upon the golden shining stairs.
The angels they will greet us there and their golden harps will play.
We will draw a million canteen checks and spend them in one day.
Tis there we'll hear Saint Peter tell us loudly with a yell.
Take front seats you boys from Guinea for you done your hitch in <u>HELL</u>.


**SC:** Who wrote that?
**DB:** I don't know. Some American boy sat down and wrote it.

**SC:** It's the truth, isn't it?

**DB:** Yes. It's the truth. Now let's see. We were finished at Biak and went into a rest area there. We were getting ready to invade the Philippines. Now, Biak was a very strategic island. It was where the bombers and everything could take off and really do damage. You know, big bombers. They couldn't come off of carriers—not the Flying Fortresses, Liberators, B-29s. They could hit the islands and do lots of damage. That was Biak Island. It was the return to the Philippines, really. MacArthur could go to the Philippines now.

We went to Mindoro Island, which was an island in the Philippines, to stage and get ready to invade a place called Zamboanga. They have a song about the monkeys have no tails in Zamboanga. And that's the truth. Some don't have tails.

**SC:** Well, they must have been baboons.

**DB:** No. They were monkeys, but they didn't have tails. And we landed in Zamboanga in March 1944. Zamboanga City is a very old city. It was an old Spanish Fortress. They had fortresses there with walls about fifteen to twenty feet thick made out of brick back in 1500, about the time that Columbus discovered America.

**SC:** Did you go in that?

**DB:** Yes.

**SC:** Was it cool?

**DB:** I don't know if it was cool or not. We went into Zamboanga as soon as we hit land. Let me tell you. We rode these little landing craft that were small and would carry two or three platoons. They were out of the water about eighteen inches, and they just rolled and tumbled. They had a bell up there that was ringing all the time because it was letting you know that it was rolling too much. But there was nothing you could do about it. But, oh, we all got seasick. And there was no feeding. All we had was something out of a can. No bread or anything like that. We just ate beef or cheese.

**SC:** Rubber cheese?
**DB:** Yeah, rubber cheese. But when we landed at Zamboanga, I was so sick, and so was everybody else. The Japs started pouring the artillery in there. But none of us really cared. We were so sick. If we got hit, it would have been a relief.

We went through a cemetery there, and it was an old cemetery. I'll never forget it. And then we went to the town of Zamboanga. We just kind of out skirted it and went on. Our objective was to take an airport that the Japs had built there. It was a pretty good airport. We took it and the next day we had fighter planes landing there, which is a great relief when you've got air protection and somebody who can strafe the enemy for you.

As we crossed the airstrip there was a Jap 75 mm artillery gun firing at us. He was firing from five or six miles away. But he could see us with his glasses. And he was shooting almost flat. He'd hit 200 yards, let's say, north of us. And then he'd raise it, trying to hit right in the middle of us, and he'd hit 200 yards below. He just kept shooting, but he never could hit right in the line. We were strung out across there. There wasn't any need to run. You might have run right into it.

Anyway, we took the airport there. So we made a circle. We came up on the Japs' fortifications there, but they had deserted them and went up in the hills.

**SC:** They were on the retreat?
**DB:** Yes. That evening, before it got dark, some Filipinos and an American woman came down out of the hills. They were missionaries. Of course, they came in to where we were setting up camp. And, of course, we were just there to fight the Japs. But I believe and I think the American woman re-

layed messages to the Japanese because that night they came in on us. And whoever it was knew exactly where we all were.

I hadn't had my shoes off in weeks. I told my buddy Burnette, "Kenny, I'm going to take my shoes off tonight because nobody's coming in on us." Just as the moon dropped behind the coconut palms, here they came.

**SC:** With your shoes off?

**DB:** With my shoes off. I was just lying up on the ground. The Japs had wrapped their feet in tow sacks so that they wouldn't make any noise. You couldn't hear them. And they got right up on us before they ran in. Well, I was lying there on my back, and I didn't know there was a Jap soldier within 400 miles. Here he came running right over me. Almost stepped right in my face. And then about that time, the machine guns, and rifles, and everything opened up, and this Jap soldier had about a half a pound of TNT tied to him. He never did see me. He was going to jump in the CP. He knew where the officers were, but someone killed him. See, at night, we shot everything that moved. Especially anything out in front of us. And if anybody was up, well, he was going to get shot, whether he was enemy or not inside the perimeter. That was a set rule. You did not get up above your hole. And that was my trouble that night. Kenny, a boy by the name of Crow, and I were all in this little swag. And the fire was going over us all right, but we couldn't get up and move. We were just there. We hadn't dug us a hole.

**SC:** You were kind of between a rock and a hard place.

**DB:** Yes. But anyhow, my shoes were off, and I broke my toe there.

**SC:** Uncle Doyle! How'd you break your toe?

**DB:** I broke it scratching and crawling around there.

## A COMMON MAN OF THE GREATEST GENERATION

SC: You must have been doing some severe scratching.
DB: Well, I was just trying to move and just slither on the ground so our own men wouldn't shoot us. And we were throwing grenades. And we never did use our rifles that night because we were inside of the perimeter.

I had a real good friend from Houston. Something happened that just tore me up. There was a barrel lying in a creek, and it had filled up with water, and in the firefight, there, Darilek was over on the opposite side of the creek from me. And somebody shot a hole in that barrel. And it was like a man choking to death in the water, and I said, "Well, Darilek and others are down in that creek, and they've hit them," you know, and I was lying there an hour or so before that barrel drained out.

The next morning when I could see, I could see what had happened. Darilek was all right, but I thought he was dead. And, you know, it was getting kind of close to the end of the war. At least we could see some hope of an ending. We didn't want to die right at the end of the war.

We were in the Philippines in Zamboanga. It was the only town, you might say, we were ever in. The rest of it, you could say, we were in jungle up until this time. We stayed around Zamboanga and the talk was: it's not going to be long until we invade Japan because MacArthur by then had Zamboanga and Biak, and he was moving up all the Air Forces and the Navy, and all of them were closing in. At that time on Zamboanga, we were up in the ridges and the mountains. We got support from the Marine Air Force and those like Albert flying in the Navy. The Marines came in with their fighter planes and gave us support.

SC: Daddy was saying that on the islands he strafed, the infantry would lay out panels of cloth. How did y'all tell them where to strafe?
DB: We would give them smoke. In the mortars, we had smoke shells and we had smoke grenades, and we had contact with the pilots. And we would tell them, "North, strafe that. But south, we're there, don't do that."

And that's the way that they communicated. We'd shoot smoke grenades or shoot mortar shells with smoke.

**SC:** When I interviewed Daddy, I asked him, "Did you ever see the jungle?" He didn't know what I was talking about because there wasn't any jungle left. It had all been blown to smithereens. But you've been the only person I've talked to that was in just horrible vegetation.

**DB:** Oh, yeah. Every day that you were in combat over there it wasn't like you could get on the battlefield in a big, huge group. It was small groups. Each company would send out platoons just inching down those little trails. Now over here around Zamboanga, it was kind of open country and we could see.

**SC:** And Zamboanga? Tell me again. Where is it?
**DB:** That's on Mindanao.

**SC:** It's the biggest island of the Philippines.
**DB:** Right. It's on the very tip. There's a town called Davao, I believe, on the eastern side of Mindanao. Zamboanga is on the very tip of the southern end of it—about mid way of the southern end. It's right on the ocean.

**SC:** Didn't you ever get a break?
**DB:** No. I never got a furlough.

**SC:** You just got over there, and you had to fight and be miserable the whole time.
**DB:** Right.

**SC:** You never got a break from it?
**DB:** Oh, we got rest areas, you know. Like on Biak, we got a month or so rest.

## A COMMON MAN OF THE GREATEST GENERATION

SC: Like in that little tent? That's supposed to be a rest area?
DB: Yes.

SC: How long were you in combat? Like in New Guinea. Like a year? Was it that long or was it six months?
DB: In New Guinea, I would say, let's see, about four to five months steady. There were breaks in there but in combat about five months, and then on Biak, about the same thing.

SC: And then you went right on to the Philippines.
DB: Yes.

SC: Like Daddy, they didn't like to keep fighter pilots out there for over six months.
DB: No, I know it. That was the unfair thing about it.

SC: You just had to stay there? Why couldn't they replace troops like they did pilots?
DB: They just wouldn't do it. The more combat you had, the more they used you.

SC: The more experience you had, I guess.

I know why they did the fighters, though, because Daddy told me that the Japanese didn't keep retraining their pilots. They never pulled their pilots out or had them retrained with people back home for support. But they did in the United States, and that's why our Air Forces all together were better because they wouldn't let all the good pilots get killed off. They'd bring them back and train new ones. And they were fresh when they went back. But it looks like they would have done that with the troops.
DB: Well, they couldn't. They didn't have enough of them.

While we were in Zamboanga, we had another mission to go around and make contact. You know, you'd be sent out to draw fire and try to find where they were.

**SC:** Stir them up?

**DB:** You didn't want to stir them up, but you wanted to find out all you could. And this was the only time we had a kind of a frontal attack. That was the first ground that we had where we could make a frontal attack. There was a good-size airport for the Air Forces. We had the whole 163rd Infantry to make a frontal attack in Zamboanga, there, and we went out in the hills. G Company, E Company, and F Company, that was all in the Second Battalion. We were in one group. G Company had some tanks, and that was the first time we ever had tanks. You couldn't run them in New Guinea. You could in Zamboanga.

We were going up a hill. E Company had taken a hill, and G Company was going around the flanks and coming up on top. The hill we were going up was for an observation post. And all of a sudden, as we started up, the whole earth just trembled. The whole earth shook, and there was a big bang. The Japs had undermined that hill. They stored all their ammunition and high-explosive stuff and bombs in that hill, and they set it off and blew E Company up—up on top of that hill. You could see E Company's men up in the air as it blew up. It didn't kill all of them. A lot of them survived that explosion.

But G Company, all we could see were huge pieces of dirt and rock, whatsoever up in the air three or four hundred feet. And G Company, none of us got hurt, but pieces of dirt and clay and whatever would be as big or bigger than an automobile coming down. We could see it coming. You could see and judge if something like a big piece of dirt or mud as big as a basket was going to hit you. Of course, we were showered with small stuff. It blew it sky high.

# A COMMON MAN OF THE GREATEST GENERATION

SC: They must have had a heck of a lot.

DB: Oh, it was. It was a terrible blast. But when they did that, we knew there weren't any Japs in there. To the Japs, suicide was an honorable way to die. That makes a fierce soldier when you've got a man that's willing to die. Americans were willing to die, but they didn't want to commit suicide.

SC: And this was getting toward the end, and they were struggling just to stay afloat, weren't they?

DB: Well, they were seeing that the thing was going to last longer than they thought it was. Once MacArthur got control of the ground and had infantry there to hold the ground, then he could start his operations. And this was really where he was getting his feet back into the Philippines. He could say, "I have returned." The Filipinos were coming out to see us and greet us. They knew that something was going to happen. The Americans had taken Leyte, Luzon, Palawan and other Philippine islands. They went into the gulf and went into Manila. They took all of that, and when they got that, MacArthur knew then that he had things going his way. He was close enough for his bombers to reach Japan. He was close enough to give fighter protection off of aircraft carriers, and things then started to take shape. We stayed in Zamboanga a few weeks.

They sent us to down south to invade the island of Jolo and the city of Jolo. Jolo was a Muslim city. It wasn't very big. It was the capital of the island. Jolo is a very old town. Probably built in the 1500s. These places are not very far from the coast of Vietnam and Southeast Asia. They had been populated for many, many hundreds of years. It was right on the equator, you might say.

SC: Was Jolo in the Philippines?

DB: I don't think the island of Jolo belonged to the Philippines. It might have, but I'm not sure.

The Muslims and the Moros were in this part of the world. We took Jolo, and I was about as scared as I ever was over there. See, these people were headhunters. When they killed you, they cut your head off and put it on a spear or something and carried it around, these Muslims. They believed in their religion: "An eye for an eye, and a tooth for a tooth." If I killed one of their brothers, then they were obligated to kill me. Under their religion, they killed you or some of your people.

SC: Now where is this place?
DB: Jolo. It's about three or four hundred miles above Borneo. They sent about ten of us to guard a lot of collaborators and elders of the city and people that ran the city as prisoners. We'd built a wire fence out in the country at a little country school. About like what Boles school [in East Texas] used to be. The old timers know what kind of school a little one-room school was. They sent us out there to guard about 200 of these collaborators.

Late that evening, these Muslims and guerillas came marching in on us. They came up and said they wanted to see their brothers and daddies, which they were, in this little compound that we had there. We knew they would just as soon fight and kill anybody. It didn't make too much difference to them whether we were Americans or not. But they did respect us. What scared me was that they were going to just slaughter all of us because we couldn't afford to start a fight and didn't have anybody to help us, But we came out of there all right. They said, "We're going to camp here tonight." Their commander said they wouldn't bother us.

SC: Well, y'all didn't hurt them, did you?
DB: No. No. But they wanted to set their fathers and brothers and all set free. They wanted to talk to them. We didn't know what they were saying. We couldn't refuse to let them talk. We were just taking their commander's word that they wouldn't harm us. There was no one there to help us, so I knew that night might be it for me.

## A COMMON MAN OF THE GREATEST GENERATION

We then went to the island of Leyte. That's where I left from. I don't know whether it picked us up or not, but I came home on the *Sea Witch*. It was May when I left there because I know I got to San Francisco in June, about the 10th or 12th, 1945. We laid over on Angel Island out there to let them test us and see if we were fit to come home. All they did was strip us off naked and run us around a big gym where there were about ten or fifteen doctors. If you could run around there, they said you could go home. It took us about three days, I believe, to come from San Francisco to San Antonio. There were so many drunk that they wouldn't process us for another day. I got out June the 15th, 1945.

SC: When was the Japanese surrender?
DB: August. Let me say this. When we were in Jolo, we were preparing to invade Japan. That was the next place. And all of my buddies or the young boys that were replacements, they all went into Nagasaki, Japan. And that's where I would have gone if they hadn't let me come home in June. I'm afraid some of the boys—especially my friend, Ross Brandt, he's having cancers right now—I'm afraid he might have been exposed to that atomic radiation.

SC: Now he wasn't there when they dropped the bomb?
DB: No. But he went in right after they dropped it.

SC: How do you feel about them dropping that bomb and making that bomb?
DB: Well, if you look at it from the standpoint of lives, you see the Japanese, they all believed in suicide, women and children and all. To die for the emperor was a sure way to heaven. They had already made up their minds that they'd die to the last human being if they were invaded. When they dropped the bombs, Hirohito said that they would

surrender. Now if we had invaded, there would have been thousands, millions killed. They figured a million or more American men would die on the island of Japan before they could make it secure for people to go in. There were maybe a half a million Japanese killed, and it was better all the way around as far as loss of life is concerned. And actually, you asked me the question about how do I feel about the atomic bomb and all that. Well, I can't see any difference from dying from being shot with a rifle or automatic weapon or artillery or an airplane dropping a bomb. I can't see any difference as far as the dying because dying is personal with everybody. If you die, it's just one individual, and it's your life. So I can't see the difference from dying from the bomb or car wreck or anything. You're dead.

SC: So you think Truman made the right decision going ahead and doing that?
DB: Yes, I think so.

SC: Some people thought we shouldn't have dropped the bomb. Some people felt the Japanese were already at the surrender stage. What I don't understand is if they were so horrible, and we had to fight them like that, why are we so interconnected with them?
DB: Now then, you've hit my sore spot now. That's what I can't understand.

SC: Hirohito died a few months ago, and the president goes over there.
DB: Right, and the good boys, fine boys, the pride of America gave their lives, and yet we're hobnobbing. I don't do that. I don't like them. I wouldn't do them any harm, but they caused me so much misery. I've had complications ever since I got out.

SC: Has the government paid for any of your complications? You haven't gone to a Veterans Hospital or anything?

## A COMMON MAN OF THE GREATEST GENERATION

**DB:** No, I got a pension for malaria for about two years. It wasn't much, but I got it. I've been thinking about going to the Veterans Hospital, but I'm on Medicare and I have insurance, and I'm at home.

**SC:** Well, I was just thinking people gave up so much of their lives to do all that, they deserve some reward for it. Not even a reward, just some care for it.
**DB:** Yes, but the government is getting where they hate to do anything. They'd rather the World War II veterans were gone, but there are still a lot of them left.

**SC:** You didn't tell me about the two times you were injured.
**DB:** Well, at Zamboanga, Odell Cates, down here, my neighbor, he was hit. They shot his stomach and kidneys, so he's never been able to work. But just a few minutes before he got hit, we were crawling up on a pill box, moving up on a big, coconut log pill box. This was in a coconut plantation. They were shooting ack-ack guns—twenty- and forty-millimeter ack-ack guns.

**SC:** Is that a Japanese gun?
**DB:** Well, that's what I call them. They were for air protection, but they'd turned this one down flat on the ground.

**SC:** Is this like an anti-aircraft gun?
**DB:** Yes, a small anti-aircraft gun. And they were using it on personnel. And they were throwing artillery, and I never knew exactly what hit me, but something hit me just like you'd hit me with a sledgehammer on my shoulder and it went between my pack and my back. It just ripped my old fatigue jacket that I was wearing. Of course, it was just wringing wet with sweat, but it just ripped it open. It just went down right over my head and right down my shoulder.

**SC:** Did it rip your skin off?

**DB:** No. It turned black almost instantly. It was so hot, and it burned the hide off, and that bloody, oozy water was coming out. I called my buddy, and he was right behind me. I said, "Kenny, I'm hit." He said, "Do you think you can get back in this ditch?" There were little irrigation ditches. I guess they were irrigating something. I said, "Yeah, I think I can get back." Well, I had my pack on. When I got back there where he was, he jerked my pack off and my shirt was ripped open and my jacket. And he said, "Well, all I can see is all the hide is knocked off and there's a knot as big as a baseball." It was as black as it could be. It felt like it was numb it hit so hard.

**SC:** You never did know what it was that hit you?

**DB:** No, I never did know, but I figure it was a piece of artillery shell that cut through there.

**SC:** What's the other time?

**DB:** We were going up the New Guinea coast there. I don't know whether I tripped it or another fellow tripped it—a booby trap. It exploded right under us. I imagine it was a hand grenade that they set off, but it just nicked my hand. I was lucky.

And I want to say this while I'm at it. All the time that I was over there in G Company, when they were in combat, I never missed a day. And it got down to where there were three of us left in my platoon. I was very fortunate that I didn't get wounded bad enough to be hospitalized or left there for dead. I never missed a day that G Company was in combat. I don't think there was another man in the company that did that.

**SC:** You must have been a healthy specimen, or just tough or something.

**DB:** I think the Lord was with me more than anything. But I was healthy. They weighed our company when we left Australia—counting the little ones, big ones—and all we averaged out 184 pounds. So you can see, there were some big men because I happen to know some of the little men.

**SC:** How much weight did you lose? Do you know? You couldn't have stayed the same weight eating what y'all were eating.
**DB:** That was the hardest thing. We never had nothing much to eat. From the time we first went into New Guinea, Sanananda, around Buna and there, to the time we got back, I lost fifty-four pounds. I was just skin and bones—really skinny, I'll put it that way—when we got back to Australia. And eaten up with malaria and other diseases.

**SC:** Let me personally thank you for your war effort. I would like to personally thank you. Most people my age have never gotten into it, and they don't understand. There'll probably never be another war like it. There never was another war like it.
**DB:** Let me say one more thing. I appreciate what you said. After the war was over, and I came back to Houston, I think I stayed two or three days in Houston or until Victor could get off and bring me up here. Well, then I met Helen, and she's taken care of me all these many years and kept me going. And she's been a wonderful wife. We've had a good life together.

**Helen Bruce:** And he never mentioned the war for years and years.
**DB:** I never said much about it. Of course, this is just brief of what all took place. You know, three years of combat, you can't put it all in there.

The war was good, and it was bad, but mostly it was bad. And I'd like to say this, as far as my religion is concerned: I am against war. And I know what the teachers and the preachers and the educators say about murder and about killing. They want to make a division there and they say if it's premeditated, it's murder and you'll have a hard time getting forgiveness for that. I understand all of that.

But getting back to the word "murder," if it's premeditated, wars are the most premeditated things that there are. They devise everything and the smartest brains in the world are making these things to kill each other. And it is premeditated. And that's the way I feel about it, and if I had it to do over, I don't know whether I'd go or not.

I was lucky and made lots of friends and I've lived a good life. All I can see is hard times for America. I don't know whether Americans today appreciate the efforts that were put forth in World War II. I know we made blunders in Korea and in Vietnam. And I'm afraid the younger Americans don't realize the wonderful country they live in. And I don't know whether they're willing to buckle down—not necessarily in war, but to make an effort, a real effort, and make it stick, to change the laws back because we have no laws. The good people now are more or less in prison rather than the bad people that are outside. Because we have to lock our doors. We lock our cars. We have to more or less guard our schools. We've got the good people practically in prison by their own choice rather than enforcing the laws. You take the foreign people that we coddle and try to help. I'm afraid it's going to destroy us, and America will be no more.

SC: There're still people like me around. There are. And your sons. And I love you.

# PART 3

# HELEN'S LETTER

October 20, 1998

Dear Travis,

I've written you about World War II and Doyle's (to some extent) part in it. He came home to Lufkin on June 15, 1945, after more than 3 ½ years in New Guinea and the Philippines under terrible conditions. I found letters that Doyle and I sent each other after we met. They are our love letters, but there is also a lot in there about what life was like after the war. I'll tell you a little about how we met, what our life was like in our early-married years, and what it was like for other young people right after the war.

I was working at Texas Foundries in Lufkin in the same office as Martha Barrington, who was the wife of Doyle's cousin, Dewey Barrington. Martha had taken a month's leave of absence to be with Dewey who was discharged before Doyle was. Martha was assistant bookkeeper, and I was the billing clerk and was also doing her work while she was on leave. Martha came by the office one day and asked me if I'd date Doyle. This was my one and only "blind" date, but it wasn't all that blind! His younger sister, Beck, and I were best friends in the fourth grade, and I knew three of his nieces in high school as well as knowing his older sisters. Martha had bought a little blue 1936 Ford Roadster while Dewey was in the service, and we double dated with them every night. I was working until 7:00 p.m. every evening, but that bothered me not at all! It didn't take Doyle long to propose, and if he hadn't been such a seemingly sincere guy, I'd have thought he was crazy!

The war ended in Europe on May 10, 1945. That was Victory in Europe Day, or VE Day, but we were still at war with the Japanese in the Pacific. Doyle got to come home in June because he had reached the number of points needed for discharge. He had been gone from home for forty-two months and never got a furlough to come home. Others did. His time in combat overseas got him the points needed.

The boys in the service from Europe wanted to come home to stay, but there were plans to send many of them to invade Japan. On August 10, 1945, we learned that Japan had surrendered. That was called Victory in Japan Day or VJ Day. The war was over! I can't tell you how excited that made us—how thankful all of us were that sons and brothers and friends had survived and would soon be home.

My brother, Albert, was still in the Navy. He was a fighter pilot on a carrier in the Pacific. He was a fighter ace. That meant he had shot down at least five enemy planes. My other brother, Leslie, had landed in Normandy in August 1944, was captured by the Germans on November 11, 1944, and spent the rest of the war in a German prisoner of war camp.

Leslie had married Lavigna before he went overseas, and he had a little boy named David he had never seen until he got home. On August 10, 1945, he had to leave Lufkin to go to the Army depot at Little Rock, Arkansas. He had asked for an extension to stay in Lufkin longer, but it was denied. Oh, how he wanted to be home with Lavigna and little David. He wired us on August 13 that he expected to be discharged soon. We were all thrilled beyond words. Soon, he and Lavigna could get to themselves. They deserved it. But it didn't happen as soon as we hoped. On the 22nd, he was still in Little Rock but was headed to San Antonio for his discharge. He was miserable that he wasn't yet with Lavigna and David. On the morning of Friday, August 24, Leslie came in with his discharge that he had gotten the day before. We were a happy lot! He was made a technical sergeant three days before his discharge. I wrote Doyle at that time, "Isn't that just like the Army? But it doesn't matter now that he is Mr. Leslie Irving Slack again."

About the same time, Albert was in Massachusetts and had orders to the West Coast to return to duty with the Naval Air Corps in the Pacific. On the 24th of August, we had gotten a letter from Albert. He said he was getting a discharge and would be home in thirty days. He flew into Beaumont and called to let us know he was coming to Lufkin. It seemed too good to be true. There were so many good things happening. It seemed too much to hope for, but four friends that had been overseas on a previous tour were all offered discharges. Albert was discharged September 8, 1945.

Finally, we were all together for the first time in years. One day in September, I wrote in a letter, "I wanted to cry all day yesterday. When I went in to dinner yesterday and saw Albert and Leslie and my whole family together again, it just sort of filled me up. I feel like I'll burst from happiness and pride. I guess I have more to be thankful for and happy about than anybody." How swell it was to have the whole family together at home and safe. That's more than we really did expect, even though we believed in God and prayer. That obviously helped more than a lot of other things.

They were such a good family. You might think we were simple how we celebrated being together again. We all went to Boykin Lake Park one Sunday for a swim and a picnic. We stayed there all day. We were almost the only

## A COMMON MAN OF THE GREATEST GENERATION

ones there. The water was exceptionally clear. Even David had a healthy swim. And the food was wonderful. We had everything from chicken and all the trimmings to ice cream and cake.

For a few weeks that fall, our family was almost like before the war. We would gather in the living room in the evenings. If the night was cool, we'd build a fire in the fireplace. We'd listen to the radio or play Albert's records on his record player. We'd drink buttermilk. Can you believe that? One night, we all went to a movie and then came home and drank cold pineapple punch. We'd talk about everything. Another night, Janice parched peanuts and Billy wouldn't go to bed until he had eaten every last one. One day in late September, Janice, our friend, Billye Marie, and I donned our slacks and walked all around Papo's eighty-two-acre farm eating huckleberries and persimmons, catching baby frogs, and picking out our Christmas 1945 tree.

It would be hard for you to imagine the state of things in this country in 1945. Prior to the war, few women worked outside the home, but now there was a need for them, and those who could went to the cities where the defense plants and factories were located and went to work. The country was changed forever. We had been involved in a war for four years. Everything had gone into the war effort. Nothing had improved on the domestic front for years. The automobiles were old, houses needed renovation, and there were few apartments or rent houses. There were no such things as the apartment complexes as you know them. Boys left for the service and returned men to marry, build homes, have children, and make better lives for themselves and their children. After the war, some women worked inside and outside of the home to help pay the bills. One other thing shared in common by the World War II veterans, most of them never talked about the war until years later.

On August 24, 1945, my parents' house got butane piped in. I was so proud of it for my mother that I could have shouted. She wasn't in great health, and it made things easier for her rather than cooking on a wood stove. And it heated the house better than the two fireplaces in the house did. The boys no longer had to cut and haul firewood all the time. It was those kind of things that might not make a difference one way or another to some girls, but they made me happy.

The boys coming home from the service didn't have civilian clothes. My brother, Albert, bought a new suit, hat, and ties in Houston. He had it mailed to Lufkin. Believe it or not, it was an exciting family event to receive and see his new suit. Those four lost war years made all those common things special. Doyle bought a new suit with a shirt, tie, hat, and shoes right before we got married. And because I loved Doyle, I had a mad fling and bought a black draped dress. It was sheer on top and had rows of sequins and looked like "Saturday Nite." I liked it. In one letter to your granddad I wrote, "I bought my lipstick and in a metal tube, by crackie!! Or did you know that we had a war that put lipstick in cardboard containers? Now wasn't that inconsiderate for all the little girls."

The discharged service men often had to return to live with their parents at first. Leslie and Albert came home to live with Papo and Mamma until they figured out what they were going to do. That made nine living in our house: Papo, Mamma, Albert, Janice, Billy, Leslie, Lavigna, David, and me. With so many adults at home, we had to share the car. That meant sometimes I didn't get to go do what I wanted to. Married couples were looking for apartments or houses. Dewey and Martha were looking for what they called a "hut." Leslie, Lavigna, and David needed their own place. Couples like Doyle and me that were about to get married were looking for places, also. Nice places to live were hard to find.

## A COMMON MAN OF THE GREATEST GENERATION

Martha was taking time off from work so she and Dewey could look for a place in Lufkin. They found an apartment near the end of September. Leslie and Lavigna got a house about the same time. It was what we called "The Pecan Orchard House" near Papo and Mamma's house. If I'd been a jealous-natured soul I'd have been envious of Martha and Lavigna. They were fixing up their homes, and it was something I was looking forward to. I was especially happy for Leslie and Lavigna. I would stop by their house on the way home from work. Their house was lovely. They had everything they needed. It was full of furniture. Of course, most of it was second hand, but they were deserving of it, and it gave me a good feeling to see them fixed so well. I always wanted them to have the best because they were such swell people, and Leslie always seemed to get tough breaks.

From the time Doyle moved to Houston on July 11 until we married on November 9, he and I wrote dozens of letters to each other. Back then, mail was the most common and cheapest way to communicate. Long-distance calls were not cheap. A first-class stamp cost three cents. Doyle and I wrote each other almost daily. Sometimes, I wrote a letter in the evening and another the next morning and mailed them together that day. We said "I love you" a thousand times, of course, and tried to plan our future lives together. We had two big questions to answer. The first was what would Doyle do to make a living? The second was where would we live? He started work again for the Southern Pacific Railroad on July 30. He didn't get his first paycheck until August 31.

I missed Doyle desperately and wanted to be with him either in Houston or Lufkin, but I wasn't idle. I frequently worked overtime until 7:00 p.m. or even 9:00 p.m. but I found time to do what I enjoyed. One favorite activity of me and my friends was going to movies. I liked to go in the afternoons and sometimes took off at noon to go to a one o'clock show. I remember going to see *Since You Went Away* with Billye Marie. I practically floated away in my own tears. I guess I was silly, but if a show is human I cry, and this one brought back the war so vividly, I didn't care if my eyes were red and squinty. I wondered what would have become of me if I'd known Doyle and loved him when he went overseas. It seemed fate had made my life the happiest anyone could ask for.

At home, there were always dishes to do, my room to clean, things to sew, books to read, letters to write, friends to entertain (girlfriends only since I now loved Doyle), David to play with, and a big family to talk to. I really didn't have to "entertain" when my girlfriends came over. We listened to music, sewed, ironed, wrote letters, talked, read, and embroidered. Everyone was too busy to have to be entertained.

The sewing and embroidering were to fill what was called a "hope chest." Back then, a young woman began preparing for married life by filling a hope chest with things that a new bride would need. Many of my hope chest items were homemade. I sewed and embroidered pillowcases, towels, washcloths, dishtowels, and napkins. I bought blankets and sheets. I expected visits from our families if we lived in Houston, so I bought a beautiful green blanket to keep them warm. My hope chest was running over. I wrote Doyle, "I hope someday you'll appreciate to some little extent the time, effort, and love I put into 'Our Hope Chest.' I don't care if I did make 'em I have some of the prettiest things. I have to take them out and put them back again at least once a week, and I'm prouder of them each time." Occasionally I washed and ironed my hope chest things to keep them clean and bright. I used Lavigna's ironing board so often, she told me she was going to give me one just like it if I ever wed. We had become close friends while Leslie was overseas. We talked about living next door to one another so we could exchange nights taking care of the kids.

## A COMMON MAN OF THE GREATEST GENERATION

As I saw Martha and Lavigna get furniture and decorate their homes, I had visions of kitchen curtains, living-room sofas, and breakfast menus for two. When Martha got her new furniture, we went to christen it. I thought it was beautiful. And Martha and Dewey were happier than they had ever been. That was the way things were. We were all glad for each other's successes. After four years of war and the postponement of marriages, homes, and purchases, it was exciting to share all that with others.

One evening, I took down the living room curtains and the shades and dusted them. I was going to put up new shades, but the new ones were smaller than the old ones, so I waited until Mamma came home from the circus to tell me what to do. We put the old ones back up. I was learning the art of cooking, but I already knew how to clean house. I was always cleaning and rearranging my room. I'd take the curtains down and dust them. I did all the fixing and decorating around the house. Mamma never bothered with it. Bless her heart. She wanted to know if I could come home once a year to rearrange the furniture after I was married.

Doyle let me know he liked biscuits. None of my recipes worked, so I decided one night I might as well learn Mamma's method. So I had her wake me early the next morning and show me what size pinch she used of each ingredient. I mixed them and made them and they were as good as hers. I did that every morning until I could cook good biscuits without her assistance. My biscuits were getting delicious, and the entire family got quite a kick out of it all, but it was fun.

I was a country girl. You would have thought I would have learned to cook long before I married. In my letters, I told Doyle he'd have to be patient with my cooking. I told him he might have to tolerate burnt biscuits. In one letter, I told him I had made the "ca-utest apron," which I was going to call a "cook apron," but I'd have to break it in starting with sandwiches and working on up until I could prepare a full meal. I added, "and Lord forgive me if I kill you."

Doyle's and my romance was not a secret for long, either at home or at work. Janice felt kind of sorry for me. She asked me who I was writing one night. When I told her "Doyle," she could only shake her head, laugh, and mutter, "Laud, Laud, it must be awful." My mother liked Doyle. She said he was solid and had good character. Those were things she always looked for, and she also said he didn't talk much. She told me he had the loveliest eyes. I looked at her with stardust in my eyes and said, "Mamma, he's just beautiful." Mamma laughed and commented she firmly believed I was in love—at last. My father had known the Bruces for ages and thought they were a swell family. To which I replied, "Well, certainly!"

Doyle tried to come to Lufkin every weekend he wasn't working. If he couldn't make it, I tried to go to Houston. If he rode the train, I'd meet his train at 5:30 on Saturday evening. We'd often get together with friends, especially Martha and Dewey Barrington. In one letter, I wrote Doyle that Dewey said he wasn't feeling well and for Doyle to bring the "hootch." Yes, your grandparents were young once and did drink a beer or two from time to time. The foundry where I worked would buy a truckload of beer in Port Arthur and sell it to employees in Lufkin. One day, Martha and I bought a case of beer and rode around with Dewey and drank a "beer or three." Lufkin and Angelina County were "dry." You couldn't buy alcohol to drink. But you could drive across the Neches River to Trinity County and purchase liquor and beer. One night, Martha and Dewey went across the river and bought some beer, but it was hot. But we sat and drank it with the little bit of ice Mamma had. It wasn't that good, but we had a great time laughing and talking while we drank it. Doyle wrote me in one letter that

## A COMMON MAN OF THE GREATEST GENERATION

he had gone to a wedding one evening. Before the wedding, he and Joe, the groom, had drunk a quart of liquor before going to the church. At the reception, Doyle "got things going" by spiking the punch. Everyone was tight, including himself. Remember, this is a story, not an example for you to follow.

In early September, Billye told me one night that she'd heard I'd be getting married soon. That news got all over town when I went into Sears and Roebuck and ordered some towels. Marguerite Martin worked there and that is how everything I did got around Lufkin. She had once told me that Doyle had asked her for a date and she didn't go. I thanked her for not going, and when she asked, "Why?" I told her she was a cute, sweet girl, and he might have liked her. I think that gave her the general impression that I liked Doyle. Later in September, I was downtown with Frank, one of my bosses. Evelyn, one of the girls who worked at the foundry, walked by and asked him when I was getting married. I hadn't mentioned anything to Frank about getting married, so naturally he answered in the negative. Evelyn said the general talk in town was that I would be married in two months. That hacked me. I began to feel like every time I made a move, people talked about it. Doyle and I weren't a very well-kept secret, I guess. You might not want to hear all that, but that's how small towns were back then.

I got mentioned in our foundry newspaper in early October. "When asked for news, Helen Slack broke out in a 'cat-swallowed-the canary grin,' and blushed prettily. We wonder why?" In the same issue, I was teased:

"'Helen says she has a 'horserace dress,'" says Billye Marie.
Martha: "What kind of dress is that?"
B.M.: "Well, it has a halter, and if the halter breaks, you don't win, you show."

I thought I'd get a lot of teasing about the second item but everyone, even the fellows in the far end of the plant, came in to personally ask if I was going to get married!

I think you'll find this funny. Your grandfather wrote me on October 15, 1945, that he had taken his weekly bath on Monday night. Good thing for a future bride to know, don't you think?

Doyle and I continued to try to decide when to marry. He teased about waiting until the fall of 1946, but neither of us wanted to wait that long. Early 1946 seemed reasonable, but really, we wanted to get married as soon as he could find us a place to live. We wanted an apartment, but I told Doyle laughingly I would be happy in one room. On Tuesday, October 30, 1945, he told me he had found an apartment. Over and over in my head I kept repeating, "Doyle has us an apartment." I didn't mean to tell anyone but my bosses, Frank and Mr. Sinnett, that we planned to be married soon, but it upset the whole office because each person who would change jobs was told I was to be married. So the whole office knew. I felt foolish and told Doyle if he didn't want to marry soon, Mr. Sinnett said I could work on indefinitely.

I began thinking of a million things. Where was the apartment? What color was the wallpaper? Where would I hang the picture of Doyle that I had just had matted and framed? My friends in the office decided that the office force would start my china and crystal. I reminded Doyle that if it weren't all given to me, we'd have to buy it ourselves. Completing your china and crystal sets was important to young brides back then. Billye, Janice, and Martha began planning a shower. Leslie and Lavigna had me over for supper. They were pleased Doyle and I were getting married and thought he was tops. Lavigna wanted to have a family reception with cake and punch after the marriage ceremony. My family was happy for us, and my mother began saving up all sorts of groceries for us. All my friends were excited and wanted to come to the wedding. In a special delivery letter to Doyle dated Monday, November 5, I reminded Doyle that my ring size was a seven. Wedding planning was well under way. Friday, November 9 was the date we planned to marry. I told Doyle I needed to know by Thursday the 8th if we were definitely getting married the 9th. I planned to quit my job Thursday and spend all day Friday getting everything together so Janice and Mamma could bring it to our apartment in Houston. I was so lucky to know such wonderful people as my family, Doyle's family, my friends, and, especially, Doyle.

I visited with Doyle's mother on Monday evening, the 5th. We talked for an hour. I liked his family. His mother had allowed me to mat and frame a picture of Doyle in his uniform. I hoped I'd get to keep it after we were married. That night, Doyle's sister, Betsy Rose, came in, and we got reacquainted. We were in the same class in high school.

One thing Doyle and I shared was faith in God. He told me that when we were married we would always continue to go to church. And we never have quit going. But we went to different churches when we met. His family went to the Church of Christ. I attended the First Presbyterian Church. Doyle's mother wanted her preacher, Brother Moody, to marry us, but I wanted my minister, Dr. McMurtry, to perform the ceremony. My religion had always meant a lot to me, and Dr. McMurtry had made it more a part of my life. He had just said the right things to give me faith when I needed it, and I had always wanted him to be the minister who married me. I had sent Doyle a copy of the first sermon Dr. McMurtry had preached after his wife died. It expressed my thoughts on religion and the right way of living. Doyle said he really enjoyed it. After my visit with Doyle's mother, she wrote him a letter expressing her desire to see Brother Moody marry us. We disagreed over the preacher to perform the wedding, but the rest of her letter was a mother's advice to live a righteous life and not partake of worldly things too much. Dr. McMurtry performed the service.

Doyle had returned to work for his former employer, Southern Pacific Railroad, in Houston and began trying to rent an apartment so we could get married after I said "yes." On Tuesday, November 6, 1945, at 9:00 p.m. (yes, I was still working overtime), Doyle called and asked if we could get married that Friday evening. The office complex became excited with planning a bridal shower for us on Thursday evening—very short notice, but what a wonderful shower it was. I received such nice, useful gifts and saw all my friends that evening.

We were married on November 9, 1945, at 6:30 p.m. in front of the fireplace in my parents' home. Just family and close friends attended. The tires on my mother's old Oldsmobile were very thin, and we decided to drive no further than Nacogdoches (twenty miles) for our honeymoon. The war was over, and the soldiers were now home as civilians. There was a festive feeling everywhere. Nacogdoches was decorated for Christmas. There was a huge decorated tree on the courthouse square in downtown 'Doches. We enjoyed it all. After the honeymoon, Martha drove us to Houston with our household shower gifts. We drove by the house where Doyle rented a room and got his clothes, and our married life began.

Within a few days in Houston, I went downtown to have lunch with an old Lufkin friend who worked for Hartford Insurance Company. Doris introduced me to her boss, and she hired me on the spot. I didn't really want to go to work, but we surely did need the money. We, as well as everyone else, thought we would live in Houston the rest of our lives, but you never know.

## A COMMON MAN OF THE GREATEST GENERATION

Doyle and I had discussed living in Lufkin. That's where we really wanted to be with our families there. Papo had 82 acres of land around his house. He constructed houses. In September, he began discussing with Leslie and Albert where he could give them land and help them build houses. He even pointed out a piece of land to Janice. But he didn't mention anything to me. That made me flat mad. Then I realized he didn't even know I was in love with Doyle. I decided a few days later if he was going to help the other kids with their houses and not offer suggestions for mine, I'd just put my own bid in. So I did at supper one night. Naturally, Papo and my brother, Billy James, kept asking what in the world I wanted with a house. Of all the dumb people! I said more in a plea than a statement, "Well, golly, Doyle and I may want a house someday. Who knows? After all, I'm not dead yet." And for the first time, Papo honestly got interested. He said we could build a helluva house for 4,000 dollars. He got me out his latest house plan, and it was awfully cute. Just right. He said a brick house would cost much more than a white cottage. I wrote all this to Doyle. Papo was such a wonderful builder. I told Doyle that my father would practically save us enough money to buy some sort of jalopy. Lastly I wrote, "all you have to do is save some money, get a job in Lufkin, and there you are. Now, how's that for me planning your life? I go to boot with the deal."

My brother, Albert, was dating a girl named Alta who taught at Colmesneil, (that's where Lake Tejas is located) south of Lufkin. Albert had always been protective of Janice and me and gave his approval to whom we dated. He approved of Doyle. Alta's parents lived a couple of blocks from Doyle's and my apartment in Houston. When Albert came to Houston to visit Alta, he stayed with us.

As you know, my dad was a masonry contractor, and there was more work than they could do in Lufkin. My three brothers were brick masons who worked for Papo, and they were considered the best in the area. Albert encouraged Doyle to take a leave of absence from the railroad and see if he liked laying brick.

After much encouragement from Albert, Doyle came to Lufkin for two months. I stayed in Houston to keep my job. After two months, Doyle decided to become a brick mason, and we moved to Lufkin. Just as Albert had said, there was brick work galore. Papo now had three sons and a son-in-law to supervise jobs and help him in every way. There were also two other masons who were just as dependable. They did the masonry work on all of the commercial buildings, hospitals, schools, churches, college buildings, as well as houses in the area. Doyle was supervising the brick and tile work on Memorial Hospital when he retired. (The hospital is undergoing a huge building program now. It is going to be a fine medical center.) After my dad retired, Doyle and my brothers continued to contract under the name of "Slack Brothers and Bruce." Albert and Leslie decided to open a lumberyard that they named Leslo Sales and my brother, Billy, and Doyle continued the business as "Slack and Bruce."

The first week we were back in Lufkin, I was walking down Main Street and I ran into an old friend who worked at the Texas Highway Department, and her boss was interviewing for a requisition clerk. I got the job—a great job.

From the time Doyle and I began talking of marriage, his dream was to have his own house. I think that was because he had to move so much as a boy. Even when he was looking for an apartment for us to rent in Houston so we could marry, he also was looking for a house to buy. His letters mentioned that frequently. He saw a few, but they were too expensive or they weren't near a bus line that we would need for transportation because

## A COMMON MAN OF THE GREATEST GENERATION

we didn't have a car. He couldn't save money as fast as he wanted so we could buy a house. That 4,000 dollars that my father said would build a fine house seemed like a mammoth amount of money that we wouldn't live long enough to save. Now that we were back in Lufkin and Doyle had a good job, we could fulfill his dream and mine. Being a wife, mother, and homemaker were my dreams.

Papo was building a small house for my grandmother and aunt who decided to move to the old homeplace instead. Papo started calling it "Helen and Doyle's house." He gave us an acre of land, and we paid him what he had invested in the house, about 3,000 dollars, and we finished it. Texas Power and Light could not get power to all the houses being built for and by veterans. We moved into and lived in our little house for three months before we had electricity. Thank goodness for butane gas that was used for cooking and heat! Kerosene lamps provided the scant light, and we bathed in a washtub in the kitchen. We took it in stride and enjoyed all the challenges. Finally, our little house was finished, and I enjoyed making curtains and turning it into a home.

Everyone wanted to see our new house, and we had company nearly every night! Our lives were and have always been busy with both of our large families, church, and friends. I had three brothers and a sister. Doyle had a brother and six sisters. Nearly all of them were living in Lufkin. Both families liked to get together for meals, parties, and such like. Many of us worshipped at the same church, the Fourth and Groesbeck Church of Christ.

We were lucky that the Slacks and Bruces enjoyed each other. Interestingly, Doyle and I were the only ones who had nearly all of both families living in Lufkin, and it kept us busy to be everywhere with everyone, especially with small children. There were a lot of children. It was a "baby boom."

## Doyle Edward Bruce

Our first son, Doyle Edward Bruce, Jr., was born on June 17, 1948. He was a beautiful, blond child. Doyle bought him a tricycle before he could walk. We turned it upside down, and he enjoyed making the wheels turn. I had quit my job before Edward was born and loved being a full-time mother and homemaker. On April 4, 1950, William (Bill) Scott Bruce was born. Nothing can be better than having two little boys who are close enough in age to enjoy playing together. Doyle and I enjoyed every minute of it. And on October 6, 1953, Paula Janice Bruce joined us. A perfect family.

Although we had added a large room and laundry room to our house, we felt the need of a larger one. We were living on Helen Street, and we built a new house one block behind us on Slack Street. It was a perfect place for children to grow up. Our neighbors, the Reads, had a son and a daughter, and the five children enjoyed their place as well as ours. The Reads had a pond, which our children enjoyed as their own.

As they grew up, Edward enjoyed the band, playing the trumpet. He always loved to read and was an excellent student. Bill played football, and we were very involved. Paula played the piano, was in the pep squad, and very social. The house was always full of boys and girls and noise.

When Edward left for The University of Texas, I went to work for the Social Security Administration just to see if my salary made a difference and if we would be as happy. We were, and I was surprised that I enjoyed working. In two years, Bill left for Kilgore Junior College, then to Stephen F. Austin University, where he graduated. Paula attended Angelina College and finished at Sam Houston University.

It all went by so fast. Doyle retired in 1978, enjoyed being with friends, making a garden, did all the errands, and learned to cook. He usually had

## A COMMON MAN OF THE GREATEST GENERATION

supper cooking when I got home from work. I retired in 1986. We had gotten reacquainted with the men he was in the service with (and their wives). They live all over the country. We have visited back and forth and really enjoy each other. We all try to make the national 41st Division Reunion, which has enabled us to see all parts of the country.

We live an extremely busy life and never seem to slow down. Well, it was so extremely hot this summer, so we did slow down some. It was too hot to get out of the air conditioning.

I'll tell you this one other story. There are events in history that are so big that you never forget where you were when they happened. We were never Kennedy people. Their father had a dream or intense desire that one of his sons would be president, and he had the money and clout to make it so. There was nothing that Joe Kennedy was not capable of doing to advance his sons. His son, John F. Kennedy, was elected president in 1960. He was rich, handsome, had a beautiful wife and two cute kids. Many of his friends were glamorous movie stars and performers. They were beginning to be more like royalty. The news media began to refer to his administration as "Camelot." He was certainly different from President Eisenhower who preceded him.

I was a den mother for Paula's Girl Scout troop. I turned on the car radio after not having it on all day. That's when I heard about the assassination of President Kennedy. Of course, the little Girl Scouts got very emotional about it. Doyle was working in Jasper. He said when they learned about it, some of the men said the SOB got what he deserved! But that was politics talking. Soon, everyone recognized what a horrible event it was. Next month's Texas Monthly is mostly about the Kennedy assassination. I'm keeping it if you ever need it.

I never got as excited about the flights in space as I did about the first American to circle the earth, John Glenn. And, of course, when man finally landed on the moon. Now John Glenn is going up again, and I'm watching it just as closely.

Love,

Grandmother

I do hope this will help. It seems terribly personal, so just use what you want. Wish you were here and we could just talk.

We wished for you last Friday evening. It was raining, and I was tired, so we drove to Ray's in the van and ate junior burgers. Yum. The best I ever ate. They taste altogether different sitting in your auto. You know Ray's didn't have a dining room to start with, just several carhops. We surely missed you and Ryan.

It started raining here last Saturday night and has hardly stopped. Everything is wet, wet. But we needed it. Hope all is well there. Give Ryan our love. Take care. Call collect if we can help you.

# ACKNOWLEDGEMENTS

Writing a book for the first time is daunting. Several individuals provided invaluable assistance to me. My friend from high school years, Marilyn Duncan, a professional editor, gave me early guidance on the process of getting a book published. She directed me to The Authors' Assistant, where Danielle Hartman Acee took me the rest of the way to the publishing of my book. She has the perfect personality and skills to assist a first time author.

My special thanks to my cousin, Sally Slack Clifton, who recorded two hours of my father's recollection of his combat experiences in World War II. These were the inspiration for this book.

Finally, I must acknowledge my best supporter and asset, my wife, Glenda. Without her love, patience, and encouragement this book would never have been completed.

Made in the USA
Coppell, TX
28 February 2024